Mountain navigation techniques

Kevin Walker

Constable London

First published in Great Britain 1986
by Constable and Company Limited
10 Orange Street London WC2H 7EG
Copyright © 1986 by Kevin Walker
Reprinted 1989
Set in Times New Roman 9pt by
Inforum Ltd, Portsmouth
Printed and bound in Great Britain
by The Bath Press, Avon

British Library CIP data
Walker, Kevin
Mountain navigation techniques.
1. Hiking   2. Mountaineering   3. Orienteering
I. Title
796.5'22   GV199.5

ISBN 0 09 466690 0

To Lesley

Contents

Contents

Illustrations

(*All photographs taken by Kevin Walker*)

Diagrams

(*Diagrams drawn by V. A. Brand*)

Introduction

Mountain navigation is not simply the art of never getting lost! It is also concerned with having the ability to find out where you are when you *think* you are lost, and then being able to get home safely. It should be seen as an aid to mountaineering and hill-walking – one small part of that indefinable skill known as 'Mountaincraft' – and not as the be-all and end-all of a day in the hills.

The most important part of successful mountain navigation is the ability to use and interpret a map. Without this basic map-reading skill, all the later-learned, so-called 'additional' techniques will be virtually useless. With practice and experience you should be able to read a map like a book: it will give you such an accurate description of the terrain that, for most of the time, there will be no need for you to use any other equipment or techniques.

Map interpretation and, more especially, some of the poor visibility techniques may sound complicated, but they are not. Navigating in the mountains is easy. The best way to learn is to take it step by step, gaining as much experience and understanding of each stage as you can before progressing to the next.

I hope that this book is written in such a way that it will allow you to follow a structured course of learning. Based upon many years' experience of running mountain navigation courses, it starts with a brief history of navigation, and then goes on to discuss maps, map reading and interpretation, and route finding. Part Three deals with compass techniques, time and distance estimation, poor visibility techniques, etc., and Part Four briefly describes the sport of orienteering – one of the best ways to practise and tone up your newly learned navigation skills.

There is one point which should be stressed from the outset: simply sitting down and absorbing the information in this book will not, in itself, make you an accurate navigator. Indeed, even if you can recite backwards every navigation book every written, you will still be next to useless when it comes to navigating in the sort of conditions where your life, and perhaps the lives of others in your group, depends on your being accurate.

There is no substitute for practical experience. Use every opportunity possible to gain as much experience as you can. When in a car, let someone else worry about the driving while you concentrate on a map. Try to work out what's coming up ahead, not just in terms of the road configuration, but more in terms of the terrain and the shape of the land. There are plenty of things you can do, even if you live in the heart of a city. Use a map to plan short walks near your home, work out what you think you are going to see, then go out and check how right you were. Who knows? You may even learn something about your neighbourhood which you had never realised before. If, at this early stage, it starts to get boring, stop. Do something else for a while and then come back to it. Navigation should be, and can be, fun!

One final point before we start. Although every effort has been made to describe the various techniques in the simplest possible way and to ensure the accuracy of all the information, I would be pleased to hear from anyone who experiences any problems or finds any mistakes.

Part one

The history of navigation

1.1 Mathematical navigation

According to *Chambers Twentieth Century Dictionary*, navigation is 'the act, science, or art of conducting ships or aircraft, etc., especially the finding of position and determination of course by astronomical observations and mathematical computations'. Mountain navigation is only one very small part of this sphere and, luckily, is nowhere near so involved. In fact, a good definition of mountain navigation would be 'the art of finding one's way around in mountains or remote areas'. It's as simple as that. However, a general overview of the history of navigation will not go amiss, if only to set the scene for what follows.

Navigation, in its simplest form, has been around for as long as man has been on this earth. As early as the Stone Age, people must have come to know local landmarks and to use them in order to get to places of shelter, water-holes, etc. But while the Ancient Britons were still running around covered in woad and dressed in animal pelts, races such as the Phoenicians, Carthaginians, Romans, Greeks, and even the Polynesians, had already started to develop somewhat more 'advanced' navigational skills due to their efforts as seafarers and merchants.

To begin with, these trading sailors followed large rivers or relied upon their proximity to the coast (both early examples of using linear features for navigational purposes), but later they began to make and use observations from the skies, both during the day and at night. The Vikings probably did most of their early navigation under similar conditions, keeping within sight of land whenever possible. Their discovery of Iceland and, some believe, America was most likely the result of being blown off course during a storm, followed by a consequent inability to get back to their home port. How two-way traffic out of sight of land first started on a regular basis is a matter for conjecture, but it is probable that some form of astral or solar navigation was used. No doubt many ships became hopelessly lost.

The situation continued like this, more or less, for some time. These could be described as the Dark Ages of navigation for, apart from minor improvements to the compass (developed from the magnetic needle of the Chinese, and still a very primitive instrument), and a growing knowledge of, and reliance upon, the observation of the sun and stars, navigation continued to be inexact and haphazard.

It was not until the Renaissance that navigation became more exact. This was mainly due to the Portuguese and, in particular, to Prince Henry the Navigator, who was involved in exploration and discovery right up until his death in 1460. The inventions and discoveries of Mercator helped to increase the accuracy of a definite north point, and it was not long before other inventions came flooding in. The 'Cross Staff' (the forerunner of the sextant) was invented by Werner at the beginning of the sixteenth century, and mathematical calculations became the norm at the start of the seventeenth century. The greatest work of this period was done by Martin Cortes, and his text on navigation was accepted as the authoritative work.

In 1675, as a direct result of a growing need for a reliable method of finding a ship's position at sea, King Charles II established the Royal Observatory at Greenwich. Latitude and longitude became bywords of sailors the world over, but there was great argument as to which meridian (or line of longitude) was the Prime Meridian (i.e. zero degrees). The British used the Greenwich meridian, the French used the Paris meridian, and so on. This was, of course, very confusing if you happened to be using a foreign map, for the values of the lines of longitude would have been different.

In 1884, at the Washington Conference (an international gathering with representatives from almost the whole of the then civilised world), it was finally agreed that the Prime Meridian should be that of Greenwich. However, the French disagreed so strongly that they continued to draw their maps to the Paris meridian and officially still do so, although nowadays most French maps make reference to the Greenwich meridian in some way.

There was (and still is) a certain amount of confusion about north. Many people did not realise that true north (the North Pole, or the most northerly geographical point on the planet) and magnetic north (the 'north' to which a compass needle points) are different places. This led to complications in the mathematical calculations needed for accurate navigation. These were increased by the sudden realisation that magnetic north, far from being a stationary point, moved about from year to year. As if this was not complicated enough, there was another problem with which the navigators had to contend.

The needle on a magnetic compass points to magnetic north by following what can be described as the 'lines of energy' of the earth's magnetic field. In a number of places around the globe, these lines of energy are distorted into curves and swirls to such an extent that, instead of leading directly towards magnetic north, they swing away in strange directions. The reasons for these major 'magnetic anomalies' are beyond the scope of this book (although minor anomalies will be mentioned in Part Three) but they caused problems for early navigators who relied upon their compasses. Instead of following a straight course, they would travel in a large curve, or zig-zag all over the place, trying to make sense of a compass which might, in some areas, do nothing but slowly spin! Eventually, no doubt, they would have reached their destination, but not by the shortest route.

Nowadays, most of the major magnetic anomalies have been charted so that allowances can be made in any course which travels through them. In addition, most planes and ships are equipped with gyroscopic compasses which are not affected by magnetic anomalies. We also know far more about the difference between true north and magnetic north. This difference is known as the 'declination' or *magnetic variation* and, because the position of the magnetic pole (i.e. magnetic north) moves around, the magnetic variation in any given area will change from year to year. At the present time, the magnetic pole is situated in the north of Canada in the region of latitude 74° north, longitude 100° west. There is also a magnetic South Pole in the region of latitude 67° south, longitude 142° east. To illustrate the fact that the magnetic pole moves around, the magnetic variation in London in 1580 was 11° 15′ east; in 1956 it was about 8° 07′ west, decreasing annually by about 07′. To illustrate the effects of a magnetic anomaly, the magnetic variation near Cape Town is in the region of 30° west!

However, these mathematical facts and figures are useless to a navigator unless he has some point of reference. To put it another way, it is no help to know that you are standing at latitude 27° north, longitude 15° west unless you know where that point occurs on the surface of the globe. Hence the science of map making (or 'cartography') developed at almost the same speed as that of mathematical navigation.

1.2 Cartography

The oldest surviving map is an Egyptian sketch of 'the roads to the gold mines', drawn on papyrus and dating from about 1300 BC. The ancient Egyptians were skilled mathematicians, as is shown by their construction of the Pyramids, and this is a surprisingly scientifically constructed map. In fact, the Egyptians estimated the size of the world so well that their assessment was not bettered until the determinations of Picard in 1671. However, this map is more of an exception than a rule for, even long after this date, most maps simply indicated, more or less inaccurately, a number of places and their supposed relative positions. A modern map, by contrast, can be extremely accurate and full of compressed information and detail.

There are six basic types of map: topographical, cadastral, atlas, general, sketch and specialist. Topographical maps are those which show physical features such as mountains and rivers and which are based upon accurate surveys. It is this type of map with which we will be most concerned. Sailors' charts generally fall into this category as they show the topography of the sea bed. Cadastral maps are of the local government type, usually on a very large scale, showing such things as constituency boundaries, the course of underground sewers and the position of street lamps. Of necessity, these are, for the most part, extremely accurate. General and atlas maps are small-scale maps upon which topographical information has had to be suppressed owing to a lack of space, and sketch maps are rough diagrams drawn mainly to give directions or relative positions. Specialist maps may be any of the above types, and contain specific information of a specialist nature: geological and archaeological maps come under this heading.

Map makers (or cartographers) have always had to contend with two major problems which they have tried to solve using a variety of methods. Firstly, because the world is spherical, it is impossible to represent it on a flat map. Globes have been seen as one answer, but even they are not totally accurate because, in reality, far from being a perfect sphere, the earth is more like a mis-shaped pear! The nearest one can come to total accuracy on a flat map is by projecting a small part of the surface on to a flat plane. Because of this, all accurate modern maps are compiled from a projection of one type of another. There are many, some of the more common being conical projection, cylindrical (or Mercator's) projection, zenithal projection and sinusoidal projection.

While the problems of representing a spherical object by projection on to a flat surface need not concern you, anyone who wishes to navigate accurately in mountainous terrain must have an appreciation of the second major problem: that of accurately portraying the three-dimensional surface of the ground (e.g. all those mountains with their ridges, spurs, valleys and cliffs) on a two-dimensional map. Before the early eighteenth century, such representation was, in general, very poor and extremely inaccurate, usually consisting of some form of pictorial symbol (e.g. little hills and mountains) with perhaps bands of different colours or shading. It was not until the idea of the 'contour line' was introduced by M.S. Cruquis in 1728 that anything like accuracy was possible.

Contour lines are defined as 'lines which join points of equal height', and are now accepted, worldwide, as the standard way of representing the shape of the land on accurate topographical maps. On certain maps (e.g. some of the old One Inch Tourist Maps from the Ordnance Survey) you may find that the contour lines have been used in conjunction with shading or 'shadowing'. Generally speaking, however, most modern maps use contour lines alone.

Both navigation and cartography are now exact sciences, but advances are still being made. Computer technology, satellites, image enhancement and laser surveying all play their part in the production of modern maps and global navigation.

When you go into the mountains, it can be said that you are going back to basics, and this applies as much to mountain navigation as it does to any other part of mountaincraft. If you have found all this talk of magnetic anomalies and lines of energy confusing, stop worrying. Mountain navigation is not complicated, even if it seems to be so at first glance. You do not have to be a scientific genius, nor do you need a high standard of mathematics. All that is required is a certain degree of concentration, a great deal of observation, a small amount of basic know-how and a simple desire to explore and enjoy the pleasures of the countryside.

Part two

Basic techniques

2.1 Introduction

This part of the book deals with maps, map reading and map interpretation, and then goes on to describe how you can put this knowledge to good use. It also briefly describes what to look for when planning your routes, and discusses what is considered to be good route finding and what is not.

Throughout both Parts Two and Three, much use has been made of practical examples taken from Ordnance Survey maps of a mountainous area. Obviously, you will find it helpful if you have these maps in front of you as you read. The maps in question are: Ordnance Survey 1:50,000 Sheet 161 – Abergavenny and the Black Mountains, and Ordnance Survey 1:25,000 Outdoor Leisure Map – Brecon Beacons National Park, Eastern Area – Abergavenny and

A selection of the more common Ordnance Survey maps used for mountain navigation. From left to right: 1:25,000 First Series, 1:25,000 Outdoor Leisure Series, 1:50,000 Landranger Series.

the Black Mountains. Both maps cover roughly the same area but show differing amounts of detail.

Although you may already have a basic knowledge of maps and map reading, it will do no harm to recap, so we will start by assuming that you know nothing at all about the subject.

2.2 What is a map?

For our purposes, the best way to describe a map is as a picture of the ground taken from directly above. Indeed, aerial photography plays an important part in the making of a modern map. It is often difficult to work out what is what on a vertical aerial photograph, either in colour or black and white. Features tend to merge with one another and, unless the sun was low on the horizon when the photograph was taken, giving long shadows, the whole landscape looks totally flat. It can also be very difficult to get a true impression of distances and scale without having some obvious point of reference.

The job of a cartographer is to take these aerial photographs, together with the results of trigonometric and other surveys, and convert all the data into a clear and usable picture of the ground. In order to be of any use, it must be an accurate picture which shows as many of the features as possible (all in their exact relative positions), tells you what is high and what is low and how steeply the ground slopes in between, and allows you to see, at a glance, the relative distances and sizes.

Cartographers have overcome many of the difficulties by using a set of symbols (known as *conventional signs*) to represent various objects and features which would otherwise be difficult to interpret. The problems of showing height and slope have been solved by the use of the *contour line*, and the difficulties of showing distance and size have been overcome by drawing the map according to a particular ratio or *scale*.

If you look at either of the maps mentioned in section 2.1 (or at any other Ordnance Survey map for that matter), you will see that there is a series of horizontal and vertical lines which divide the map up into squares of equal size. The lines are known as *grid lines*, and the squares (naturally enough) are called *grid squares*. Each line has a number, the numbers being printed around the borders of the map, and by quoting these numbers in a particular way, it is possible to pinpoint the position of any feature or object, anywhere in the country, with great accuracy.

To recap: a map is a picture of the ground drawn in such a way that it gives a clear and accurate description of the landscape and features. The better the map, the clearer and more accurate it will be.

Let us now look at each of the features of a map in more detail.

2.3 Scale

People often get confused by the idea of scale, although the concept is quite straightforward. A scale of 'one inch to the mile' simply means that a distance of 1 in on the map represents a distance of 1 mile on the ground. Therefore, if you take a ruler and measure the distance between two objects on the map, you can work out how far they are apart on the ground. For example, if you find that two objects are 5½ in apart, you know that, travelling in a straight line, you would have to walk 5½ miles to get from one to the other.

Almost all Ordnance Survey maps have now been converted to the metric system, so you will have to get used to using centimetres, metres and kilometres instead of inches, yards and miles. If you are used to the old, Imperial system of measurement, you may find the conversion a little difficult initially, but it is worth persevering because the metric system is far easier to use in mountain navigation once you have become familiar with it.

Scale is almost invariably stated as a ratio. This figure may look complicated, but it's not. For example, a scale or ratio of 1:50,000 simply means that one unit of length on the map (e.g. 1 cm) represents 50,000 units of length on the ground (e.g. 50,000 cm, which is equal to 500 m or 0.5 km). Thus, at a scale of 1:50,000, a distance of 1 km on the ground is represented by a distance of 2 cm on the map. One of the easiest ways to remember what the ratio means is to change the ':' to a '=' (e.g. 1 = 50,000).

The main area of confusion usually revolves around the difference between 'large-scale' and 'small-scale'. Perhaps the best way to explain this difference is to say that the larger the scale of the map, the more detail it will show. Because one needs space to show details, a large-scale map of 50 cm square will cover a smaller area on the ground than a small-scale map of the same size (see Fig. 1).

On a 1:25,000 scale map, 1 cm on the map represents a distance of 0.25 km on the ground (1:25,000 means the same as 1 = 25,000; 25,000 cm equals 250 m or 0.25 km). Therefore, a distance of 1 km on the ground takes up 4 cm on the map. On a 1:100,000 scale map, the same distance of 1 km only takes up 1 cm on the map. Thus the smaller the number after the '1', the larger the scale of the map, and the greater the amount of detail that can be shown.

The two most commonly used scales for mountain navigation are 1:50,000 and 1:25,000. The 1:50,000 scale maps are probably the more popular because each map covers a greater area, and therefore fewer maps are needed to cover a particular region. At one time, the 1:25,000 scale maps each covered an area of only 100 km² and, during a good day's walking, it was possible to 'walk off the map'! This meant it was necessary to take along a number of these maps in order to cover the complete area to be walked, plus a little extra just in case you got lost and 'fell off the edges'.

However, the Ordnance Survey are now producing a new series of 1:25,000 scale maps, each one covering twice the area of the old sheets. They also produce special 1:25,000 Outdoor Leisure Maps of all the major mountain areas in Britain, each one covering an area of approximately 550 km². This means that the larger scale maps are becoming increasingly popular, and justifiably so, for they are undoubtedly far superior when extreme accuracy is needed, as in mountain navigation.

Whichever scale you use, you should always ensure that there is no possibility of your walking off the map, even if you get lost. If your proposed route goes anywhere near the edge of the map, take along the adjoining sheet. Ideally, you should gain experience of

1:50,000

1:25,000

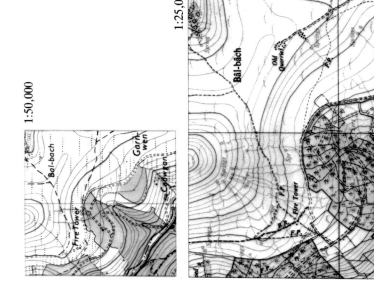

Fig. 1. Scale. These two map extracts cover exactly the same area on the ground. Note how, as the scale gets larger, the figure after the '1:' gets smaller, and the size of the map and the amount of detail increases. Note particularly the detail with regard to tracks, field boundaries, and streams. (*Ordnance Survey maps Crown Copyright reserved*).

using both scales, and until you can tell them apart at a glance, you should always check which scale you are using: there is a big difference between them. If you normally use the 1:25,000 scale maps, and you are trying the 1:50,000 scale for the first time, you will be (pleasantly) surprised by the difference in the representation of distance, and by the greater amount of detail shown.

To recap: scale is simply the cartographer's way of representing distance and size. A scale of 1:50,000 means that one unit of length on the map represents 50,000 of the same units of length on the ground. If you have any difficulty understanding the ratios, try changing the ':' to a '='.

2.4 Conventional signs

Conventional signs are a form of shorthand used by cartographers to represent various features, both obvious (roads, streams, buildings) and less obvious (parish boundaries, county boundaries, spot heights, battle sites). The symbols are fairly standard throughout the Ordnance Survey maps in common usage for mountain navigation and, in any case, are always described on each sheet, either at the side or the base, or on the back. A selection of conventional signs is shown in Fig. 2.

While it is unlikely that you will ever need to recognise all of these symbols for mountain navigation, you should certainly try to learn the more common ones so that you can recognise them immediately without having to keep on referring to the key. For example, it is rare to need to know the difference between a church with a spire, a church with a tower and a church with neither. It is more important in the context in which you will be using the map to know the conventional sign for a cliff or a steep slope, and to be able to recognise which is the base and which the top.

You should also know which symbols represent features which you can actually find on the ground. It goes without saying that you should not expect to find any sign of a parish boundary as you wander across the mountains, even though it is marked clearly on

Conventional signs

GENERAL FEATURES

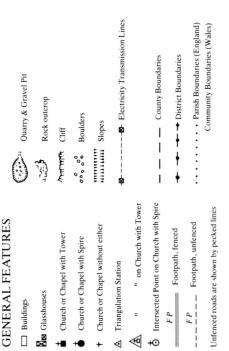

□ Buildings

Glasshouses

Church or Chapel with Tower

Church or Chapel with Spire

+ Church or Chapel without either

△ Triangulation Station

" on Church with Tower

" on Church with Spire

Intersected Point on Church with Spire

F P ═══ Footpath, fenced

F P ╌╌╌ Footpath, unfenced

Unfenced roads are shown by pecked lines

Quarry & Gravel Pit

Rock outcrop

Cliff

Boulders

Slopes

Electricity Transmission Lines

County Boundaries

District Boundaries

Parish Boundaries (England)

Community Boundaries (Wales)

WATER FEATURES

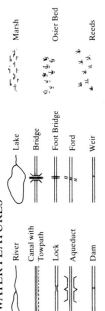

River

Canal with Towpath

Lock

Aqueduct

Dam

Lake

Bridge

Foot Bridge

Ford

Weir

Marsh

Osier Bed

Reeds

HEIGHTS

Contours are at 25 feet vertical interval shown broken in built up areas.

123 Spot Height

PUBLIC RIGHTS OF WAY

Public Paths { Footpath / Bridleway

Road used as a public path

Fig. 2. Conventional signs. This selection of a few of the conventional signs used by the Ordnance Survey has been taken from a First Series 1:25,000 Outdoor Leisure Sheet (*Crown Copyright reserved*).

the map. Admittedly, you may find a boundary stone, cairn or marker post, but they will be shown on the map with their own symbols. It is especially important that you can tell at a glance the difference between a boundary and a footpath; many beginners have spent a futile half-hour searching for a footpath that never existed, all the time crossing and recrossing a boundary. In this type of situation, without realising what you are doing, you can easily think yourself lost when you are not.

One of the more common mistakes so far as conventional signs are concerned is in the interpretation of the 'field boundaries' shown on the 1:25,000 scale maps. These grey (or black) lines do *not* represent dry stone walls. They represent, as is said, field boundaries, which can be a wall, a hedge, a fence, a ditch or an earth bank. There may even be no physical feature to represent the boundary on the ground, the landowner having demolished it since the map was published.

This brings us to another important point: the age of your map. This is easy to check as every Ordnance Survey map has its latest revision date printed in the key. Although mistakes are comparatively rare on the Ordnance Survey's maps, any map is out of date as soon as it is printed. It may well be that, since your map was produced, a farmer or other landowner has demolished a fence, grubbed up a hedge or divided a large field into two. While dry stone walls tend to be fairly permanent features in any mountain landscape, you still have to be careful. There are many other changes that may have taken place since the cartographer first saw the aerial photograph and the survey results. A new housing estate may have been built in the valley, a road may have been improved by having its corners straightened, a high mountain valley may have been dammed to form a reservoir. The possibilities are countless: mature forests are felled, new forests are planted, footpaths become overgrown and disappear through lack of use. If the map is old enough, you may even find that a river has altered course. All this means that an awareness of the static nature of a map and the dynamic nature of the landscape is of paramount importance.

Another common problem concerns the meaning of the conventional sign for a 'Public Right of Way'. The presence of this symbol on the map does not necessarily mean that there is a well defined footpath on the ground. Where this symbol and the symbol for a footpath are superimposed, you will generally find some form of path (unless it has become overgrown through lack of use), but if the 'Right of Way' symbol appears by itself you should be aware that there may not be any path.

In general, you should always trust your map first and your judgement second, but it is important to realise that your map can be wrong. If you are ever in doubt, ignore the lesser features, and try to work out the shape of the land from the map. It is, after all, the shape of the countryside (the topography) which tends to be the most stable component. Luckily, in Britain, we do not suffer from major earthquakes, and those factors which do affect topography (such as landslip, quarrying, open-cast mining) tend to be fairly obvious.

If you are to work out the shape of an area accurately from your map, you must be able to interpret a very important conventional sign – the contour line.

To recap: conventional signs are a form of shorthand used by cartographers to represent both obvious and not-so-obvious features on the ground. Since the map was published, some of these features may have been altered, or even disappeared altogether.

2.5 Contour lines

A map is obviously a flat piece of paper, but the countryside is very rarely totally flat, especially in the areas in which you are likely to be walking! There will be mountains and valleys, ridges, spurs, cliffs, all manner of depressions and hillocks, and an infinite variety of other 'ups and downs'. Cartographers represent these vertical differences by the use of a conventional sign known as a *contour line* (or simply *contour* for short).

It bears repeating that contour lines are defined as 'lines which join points of equal height'. These are the lines (usually coloured light brown) which form the patterns on your map, and it is extremely important that you understand the lines, and equally essential that you learn how to interpret the patterns made by them. This is, some say, the most complicated part of map interpretation. It is also arguably the most important, and if you can master this one idea then you are well on your way to being a successful and accurate mountain navigator.

An experienced map reader is able to look at the contour patterns and 'see' all those features mentioned above: the mountains and valleys, ridges and spurs. Not only this, he will also be able to see the exact shape of the slopes: where they are steep, where they are gentle, whether they are smooth or stepped, regular or irregular, and so on. In short, he will know, in advance, exactly what shape the land will be over the next horizon.

Each contour line on the map represents a certain height on the ground. Because the lines join points of equal height, all points lying along the same line will be at exactly the same height above sea level. The difference in height between points on one contour line and points on the next is known as the *vertical interval*, and it remains constant over the whole of the map. Therefore, if your map has a vertical interval of 10 m, you know that all the points on one particular contour line are 10 m below all those points on one contour line above it, and 10 m above all those points on the contour line below it. The height or value of the vertical interval varies according to the scale of the map, but will always be stated in the key. Vertical interval is illustrated in Fig. 3.

You will remember that earlier it was stated that the larger the scale of the map, the more detail it could show. This applies just as much with contour lines. The more contour lines there are for every 100 m of height, the smaller the vertical interval between them. Thus the shape of the various 'ups and downs' of the landscape can be shown far more accurately and with greater detail the smaller the vertical interval.

Whatever the vertical interval, there are certain rules, patterns and shapes which are basic to the understanding of contour lines. Perhaps the most basic of these rules is that the closer the contour lines are to one another, the steeper is the slope of the land. This is easily explained. If, for example, the steeper is the slope of the land. This is

Contour lines

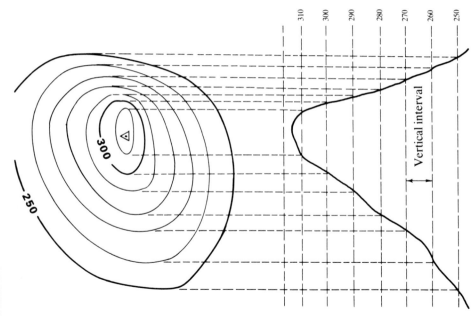

Fig. 3. Vertical interval. This diagram shows a vertical interval of ten units. Note how the figures on the contour lines always 'face uphill'.

there are five lines shown in a horizontal distance of 1 km, it means that the land rises by 50 m over that distance. If, however, there are twenty such lines in the same distance, it means that the land rises by 200 m, and must therefore have a steeper slope.

One of the simplest ways in which to illustrate how contours work is with a handful of coins. Place a ten pence piece on a flat surface, then place a two pence piece centrally on the top of it. Follow this with a five pence piece and then a penny. If you now look coins from one side, you will see – with a little imagination – that they form a conical, stepped 'hill'! Now look at the coins from directly above. Notice how the rims form a series of concentric circles. The top of each coin is a form of contour line which marks the height of each coin rim above the surface on which they are resting. The thickness of each coin is its vertical interval. However, it is unlikely that you will ever find a hill shaped like a pile of coins. Moreover, because the coins are of different thicknesses, the vertical interval of the contour lines is not constant as it is on maps. So let us now go one stage further.

Find a large, oddly shaped potato – the larger and more oddly shaped, the better. Cut it in half along one of its long axes and discard one of the halves. Now cut the remaining half into a number of equally thick slices, cutting along exactly the same plane as before. Place all these slices, in order, one on top of another, on a flat surface (see Fig. 4). Looking at your half potato from one side, you will see what could be imagined as a strangely shaped hill. Looking at it from directly above, you will see a number of lines, one between each slice. These lines are its contour lines, and the thickness of each slice is the vertical interval. On maps, the contour lines represent the lines between equally thick imaginary slices of land.

By experimenting with your potato 'hill', cutting out grooves to represent valleys, forming ridges and spurs, etc., you will begin to see which patterns represent what shapes on the ground. It is a good idea for you to have handy a map of an area that you know well so that you can compare potato patterns with similar patterns on the map.

What you will soon begin to notice, no doubt, is that certain

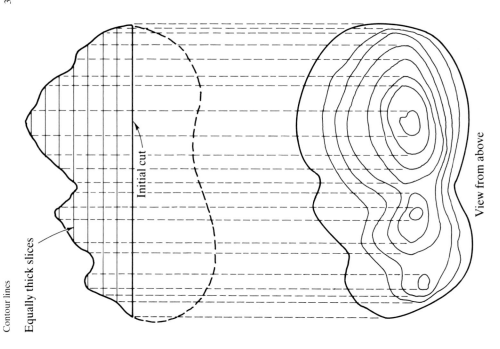

Contour lines

Equally thick slices

Initial cut

View from above

Fig. 4. The 'potato hill'.

features which are totally different from one another produce markedly similar patterns of contour lines. For example, there seems to be little difference between the patterns representing valleys and those representing spurs, and a smooth slope going up to the left can look exactly the same as a smooth slope going up to the right. In order to differentiate between these similar patterns, you must be able to work out which way the slope faces (in other words, you must work out the *aspect of slope*, or which is the top and which is the bottom). There are a number of ways in which this can be done.

In areas where space permits (where the contour lines are not too close together, or where there is a lack of any other surface features), some of the contour lines will be labelled with the height they represent. One small problem that you will meet in this context is that the Ordnance Survey are at present (1986) in the process of converting all their maps to the metric system, so some sheets give heights in feet, whereas others (the more recent revisions) give heights in metres. You can check which is which by referring to the map's key.

The figures printed on the contour lines serve a dual purpose. Firstly, they tell you the exact height above sea level which is represented by all the points on that line. Secondly, they tell you the aspect of slope, for the figures are always written with their tops pointing uphill.

Another way in which you can work out the aspect of slope is by looking at the natural drainage of the area. After all, rivers don't flow uphill, neither are they usually found flowing along the tops of ridges or spurs! It is usually fairly easy to work out the direction of flow in mountainous areas, for most streams start at the heads of mountain valleys and cwms. If this is not immediately apparent you will have to trace the course of the stream until you find either its source, or its confluence with a larger river.

Various other methods can be used. *Triangulation pillars* (or *trig points*) usually occur at the high points of a particular area, and *spot heights* can be compared. Both of these are represented on the map by conventional signs and are, of course, mentioned in the key. Spot heights, like boundaries, have no actual representative feature

An Ordnance Survey triangulation station or trig point. These features can be an extremely useful aid to pinpointing your location in otherwise featureless terrain. Location = SO/147159. View approximately 300° Mag.

on the ground – they are simply surveyed heights. Trig points, however, can be extremely useful when navigating. A trig point is a four-sided concrete pillar, slightly wider at its base than at its top, and usually about 1.5 m high. They are used by cartographers as an aid to their extremely accurate surveying techniques. The reason they are so useful in mountain navigation is that, when you are standing by one, you should know your exact position (unless you are standing at the wrong trig point!).

Because contour lines join points of equal height, the lines should theoretically be endless, appearing as misshaped circles. After all, you cannot have a point with no height, nor can you have a height which suddenly disappears. However, particularly in mountainous areas, where the slopes can be very steep, you may find that the contour lines suddenly stop, only to be replaced by the conventional sign for a cliff or a steep slope. This is because, if used, the contour lines would be so close together that it would be impossible to distinguish between them. Indeed, if the cliff is vertical and of great height, the contour lines would be one on top of another. The conventional signs for cliffs and steep slopes allow you to distinguish between the top and bottom of the crag, and are therefore very important signs.

Some examples of contour line patterns and the shapes they represent are shown in Fig. 5. Once you are able to interpret the patterns made by a series of contour lines, you should start to appreciate the importance and meaning of otherwise insignificant 'little squiggles' on single contour lines.

2.6 Grid references

It is often useful, and sometimes necessary, to pinpoint a feature or

To recap: contour lines are conventional signs which indicate height. When used in conjunction with one another, they indicate the shape of the land. It is therefore very important that you understand them, and are able to interpret the patterns made by them.

Grid references

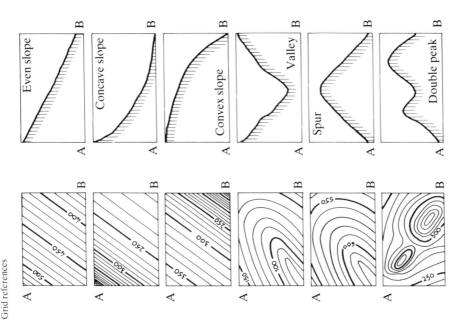

Fig. 5. Contour patterns. This diagram shows various contour patterns and the corresponding topography. Try covering either column and work out the shapes or the patterns for yourself. You might like to handy a map of an area you know well so you can compare the examples with actual patterns on the map.

position for someone's else benefit, or even for your own future reference. To do this by descriptive means would take a long time and, unless you wrote reams of notes, would only be an approximate location. There is, however, a system, based upon the National Grid, whereby you can quickly and easily locate any position in the country with great accuracy. This uses a series of figures (and sometimes letters as well) known as a *grid reference*.

The National Grid is composed of two sets of imaginary parallel lines (known as *grid lines*), one set running roughly north to south, the other – at right angles to the first – running roughly west to east. In both sets the lines are exactly 1 km apart, and each line is numbered, the numbers running from 00 to 99 and then being repeated. You will remember from the section on the History of Navigation that the north to which a compass needle points is different from the north of the North Pole. You were introduced to the idea of two different points, one called true north, the other called magnetic north. There is now another point for you to remember, this one being *grid north*. This is the north to which the grid lines point, and will be discussed in greater detail later. It is mentioned at this point because it is very important you appreciate that there is more than one north.

The method by which you work out a grid reference is very simple, as long as you follow a few basic rules. These rules are in fact printed in the key of every 1:50,000 and 1:25,000 scale Ordnance Survey map, so you can always check whether you are quoting the reference in the correct order until you become familiar with the procedure.

If you look at any 1:50,000 or 1:25,000 scale Ordnance Survey map, you will see that it is divided into squares by two sets of parallel lines. These are the grid lines, and their reference numbers are printed around the borders of the map. Grid north is always at the top of the map. Because these lines are always exactly 1 km apart on the ground, each square formed by them covers an area of exactly 1 km, the size of the square *on the map* being dependent upon the scale. If you refer back to Fig. 1 you will see this illustrated quite clearly.

If you wish to give a very approximate location of an object, you

Grid references

can do so by giving the grid reference of the grid square in which it lies. This is known as a 'four-figure reference', and locates the object to within the area of the grid square which, as has been pointed out, is always 1 km², no matter what the scale of the map.

To work out a four-figure reference you should proceed as follows. Run your finger up (or down) the line which forms the *left* edge of the square in which the object is situated, until you reach the top (or bottom) of the map. This line will have a two-figure reference number (e.g. 21). Make a note of this number, then run your finger to the left or right along the line which forms the *base* of the square in which the object is situated, until you reach one side of the map. This line will also have a two-figure reference number (e.g. 04). The grid reference for that particular square is the first number (21) followed by the second number (04). The four-figure reference of that square is therefore 2104. Remember that you must always quote both the figures in any line's reference number. You can never have a three-figure reference; indeed, all grid references always have an even number of figures.

When giving any grid reference you must always start with the figures printed along the top or bottom of the map, and follow these with the figures printed up the sides. There is an easy way to remember this: *Go along the corridor before going up the stairs*. In other words, always quote the numbers printed along the top or bottom of the map *before* you quote the numbers going up the sides.

Below are some examples of four-figure references taken from Ordnance Survey 1:50,000 Sheet 161 (Abergavenny and the Black Mountains). You may like to have this map in front of you so that you can have a practical example of how these four-figure references are calculated.

Pwll Gwy-rhoc = 1815   Llangynidr = 1519
Maen Llwyd = 2227   Sugar Loaf = 2718

If you now check these four places on your 1:25,000 scale map of the same area, you will see that the four-figure references are exactly the same. This means that once you have a grid reference for an object, that grid reference remains the same, no matter what

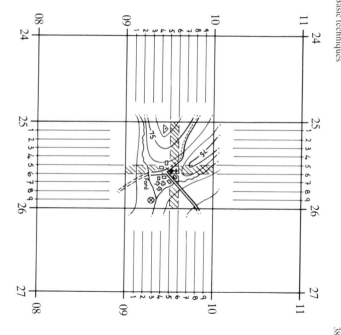

Fig. 6. Grid references. To calculate a grid reference correct to six figures (using the church as an example):

1. Find the number of the grid line to the left = 25
2. Estimate number of tenths away from this line = 5
3. Find the number of the grid line below = 09
4. Estimate number of tenths away from this line = 5

The six-figure reference of the church is therefore 255095 (i.e. it lies in grid square 2509, and is five tenths of a square across from line 25, and five tenths of a square above line 09).

What are the grid references of the trig point and the stream junction (marked 'x')?

Answers: Trig point = 250094. Stream junction = 258093.

the scale of the map.

A four-figure reference locates a point to within a 1 km square, but you will usually wish to be far more accurate than this. The standard method is by using a six-figure reference which locates a point to within a 100 m square. This grid reference is calculated using exactly the same method as that outlined below, the first, second, fourth, and fifth figures referring to the grid square in which the object is located. Thus a feature with a six-figure reference of 107492 would have a four-figure reference of 1049. This is simply another way of saying that it lies in grid square 1049. The third and sixth numbers (in our example the 7 and the 2) locate the position of the feature within its grid square.

The third figure (7) indicates that the object lies seven tenths of a square *east* of line 10; the sixth figure (2) indicates that it lies two tenths of a square *north* of line 49. Thus, by giving the grid reference of the square in which a particular feature lies, and including in that reference an estimation of tenths of a square (or decimal places) to the east (for the third figure) and the north (for the sixth figure), you can locate any feature to within a 100 m square. Remember that the top of your map is north, the bottom is south, the left edge, west, and the right edge, east.

Fig. 6 shows graphically the calculation of a six-figure reference. It also shows quite clearly that, contrary to popular belief, a grid reference refers to an area and *not* to a point. People who mistakenly believe a grid reference to be a point often make mistakes when calculating six-figure references. The mistake usually occurs when the point lies close to one of the grid lines. If, for example, a point lay slightly to the east of grid line 25 (neither exactly on it, nor one tenth of a square away from it), a common mistake would be to give it a reference of 251***, simply because it was not lying on the grid line. In fact, the reference should be 250*** because it is situated less than a tenth of a grid square to the east of the line. This should be clear if you refer to Fig. 6. All you have to remember when calculating the tenths, no matter whether you are calculating them from the north-south lines or the east-west lines, is that if a point is less than a tenth away from the line the figure is 0.

Basic techniques

Below are some examples of six-figure references taken from Ordnance Survey 1:50,000 Sheet 161.

Llwyncelyn = 161189   Junction of paths = 204286
Trig point = 262226   Garn-wen Cairn = 280255

As before, you can compare these on the equivalent 1:25,000 scale map if you like.

In some situations (e.g. if you have a hobby such as geology or botany), you may wish to be even more accurate. This can be done by giving an eight-figure reference which locates a point to within a 10 m square, but to give one at all accurately you really need to be using a 1:25,000 scale map. The procedure is exactly the same as before, except that you have to estimate to two decimal places instead of one (i.e. you work out hundredths of a square!) However, in terms of general mountain walking it is usually unnecessary to be this accurate, and most people will find that six-figure references are ideal.

If you are quoting a grid reference of a point or position from some other part of the country, or storing one for future reference, or even sending a rendezvous position to a friend, you would be wise to quote the number of the map from which it was taken. To be absolutely correct, you should quote the *grid letters* for that reference, which are shown in the map's key. The reasoning behind this is quite simple. Each set of grid lines, numbered from 00 to 99, is repeated at intervals of 100 km across the country. Each set therefore has a letter to distinguish it from its neighbours. A standard six-figure reference is unique for the map from which it was taken, but owing to the fact that these numbers do repeat themselves, it will recur at intervals of 100 km all over the country. It is rarely necessary to quote the grid letters, but if you want a truly unique grid reference you should place them in front of the figures (e.g. SO/294306).

To recap: a grid reference is a way of pinpointing (more or less) any object, feature or position, anywhere in the country. It is calculated according to a set procedure, with reference to the grid lines printed

40

on every map. You should always quote the numbers printed along the top or bottom of the map before quoting those running up the sides. Remember also that a grid reference is a square and not a point.

All Ordnance Survey 1:50,000 and 1:25,000 scale maps give an example of how to calculate a six-figure reference. Until you are perfectly familiar with the procedure, you can check that you are quoting the figures in the correct way. With practice, you will find using grid references both quick and easy.

2.7 Map interpretation

It was said at the beginning of this book that the most important part of accurate mountain navigation is map reading. This was, perhaps, a little simplistic, for the ability to read a map is not quite enough. You need to go a stage further and develop an ability to *interpret* a map, and map interpretation can only be learned through practical experience. In severe, perhaps white-out, conditions, when you are not quite sure where you are, having the ability to interpret your map can become a matter of life and death.

Map interpretation is a two-way process: not only should you be able to tell the 'lie of the land' from the map, you should also be able to use the shape of the country around you to enable you to find your position accurately. It is the latter point, in particular, that usually requires some practice.

Five of the most important considerations in accurate map interpretation can be remembered by using the mnemonic CROOK. The C stands for concentration, the R for reasoning, the two Os for observation and organisation and the K for knowledge. These apply equally to mountain navigation in general, and are described in detail at the beginning of Part Three.

The most important difference between map reading and map interpretation can be explained by the example of someone reading a book written in a foreign language. A person with a small working knowledge of that language could read the book, referring to a dictionary every now and then, and, after a fair degree of effort, could glean a basic understanding of what the book was all about. A native of that foreign country, however, would understand the book far better, appreciating some of the more subtle phrases, and gaining an overall 'feel' for the book on first reading. If the book contains long or unusual words, even he may have to refer to a dictionary on occasions.

The person with the small working knowledge can be likened to the map reader, his dictionary being the equivalent of the map's key. The native is the equivalent of the map interpreter, who will get an overall 'feel' for the land as soon as he opens the map, and who will be able to appreciate the subtleties of the contour lines and other conventional signs. Someone who is good at map interpretation will 'see the land' instead of seeing a mass of colours and lines and symbols.

So how does map interpretation help you when you are on the hill, and how can it be used effectively? Perhaps the best way to illustrate this is by giving some practical examples.

Let us assume that you are not quite sure where you are, apart from the fact that you are standing on the slopes of a particular mountain. Obviously (and certainly to begin with) it would be helpful if there were a few definite or recognisable features nearby, so let us further assume that you have no idea where you are on this mountain apart from the fact that you are standing at the junction of two streams. Straight away, things are not as bad as they could be: at least you know which mountain you're on, and you have a definite point of reference (the stream junction) from which to start trying to work out your exact position.

Looking at your map, you see to your dismay that there are several stream junctions shown in what you believe to be your approximate area, and you suddenly realise that you could be standing at any of them. This is the stage at which map reading becomes ineffective and map interpretation takes over. Exactly what you do now will depend upon the situation at the time. You can either look at each stream junction shown on the map in more detail, or you can look at the shape of the land around you, trying to fit this shape to the stream junctions shown on the map. In practice, you will probably use a combination of both techniques. In the case in question you are lucky, because you notice a substantial crag on the spur lying above the stream junction, and you see on the map that only one stream junction is situated below a spur which has a crag. You must, therefore, be standing at that stream junction.

Admittedly, this is a very simple example, but it does serve to illustrate a couple of points. Firstly, simple common sense should tell you that you should never be so lost that you can't make some form of approximation of your position (and, after all, mountain safety is basically common sense); and secondly, it is far, far easier to work out your position when you are standing at (or near) some identifiable feature than it is if you are standing 'in the middle of nowhere'. If you find yourself in the latter situation, it is often easier to carry on for a while until you reach a definite feature than it is to locate yourself simply by comparing the shape of the land around you with the contours on the map. However, you should *not* carry on if you can't see where you're going, or if you are in a potentially dangerous situation (e.g. near steep and/or rocky ground with mist closing in). Obviously, if you happen to be standing in a shallow basin, your view is going to be very restricted, in which case you should walk to slightly higher ground from where you can see far more. The more you can see, the easier it will be to compare with the map, and the easier it will be to find your position.

Wherever you are, there will almost certainly be something you can identify, whether it is near or more distant. Look at the features around you (such as lakes, stream junctions, sheep enclosures, patches of woodland). Use this information in conjunction with your observations during the previous half-hour and – most important – with the shape of the surrounding land. By comparing what you can see with what is shown on the map, you should be able to work out exactly where you are. This task will be made much easier if you can turn (or *orientate*) the map in such a way that the features to the left and to the right of you appear as left and right on the map as well. This procedure is known as *setting the map*.

In certain circumstances (when, for example, you are walking in featureless terrain, or suffering under conditions of extremely poor

visibility) it may be very difficult, or even impossible, to set your map without the aid of a compass. This technique will be described in Part Three. However, it is usually possible to set the map by eye alone, especially if your map interpretation is good, and you have been observant during your walk. As with all the other techniques in this book, you should practise setting the map by eye whenever you can, certainly until you find the procedure relatively simple and straightforward.

What is needed is some feature (or better still, a combination of a number of features) which is obvious both on the ground and on the map. The best features for this are *linear features*, such as roads, rivers, edges of forests, field boundaries or lines of electricity pylons – in fact, anything which runs, more or less, in a straight line. All you have to do is turn the map in such a way that the feature shown on the map runs in the same direction as the feature you see on the ground. To begin with, you may find that you get a few totally back to front (or 180° out), but this mistake should become quite apparent when you start to compare other features.

Where you cannot find any linear features, try to get a combination of at least two, preferably three, other features. For example, you may have a definite mountain peak directly in front of you and a stream junction to your left. In this situation you would turn your map so that the features shown on the map appeared in corresponding positions: the mountain peak would be towards the part of the map furthest from you, and the stream junction would be towards the left.

Once you have set your map correctly, all the features that you can see on the ground will appear in corresponding positions on the map, and vice versa. In other words, everything will 'fit'. A correctly set map will have its northern edge pointing north.

Let us now take a look at a couple of totally hypothetical examples which illustrate the helpfulness of setting the map.

In the first example, you have been strolling around a reasonably

The 'Tommy Jones' obelisk on the slopes of Corn Dû. Features like this are often marked on your map, and can be used in exactly the same way as trig points to pinpoint your position. Location = SO/000217. View approximately 280° Mag.

safe area for some time when you notice nasty-looking clouds on the horizon. You decide to get back to base by the shortest feasible route, but the problem is that you only know your approximate position. It appears, from the speed of the clouds, that you are going to be caught whatever you do, therefore you want to work out your exact position before the visibility becomes too poor. Once you know your precise location, you will, as we will see in Part Three, be able to negotiate your way back to base, safely and with little difficulty, no matter how poor the visibility becomes.

You notice, a short distance away, a small pool with a stream leading from it. This is your definite feature, and you move close enough to allow you to note any distinguishing features which you might identify on the map. You note, from the map, that there are four pools in your area, but one of them can be ruled out because it has no stream issuing from it, and another can be discounted because it is totally the wrong shape. This leaves you with two possible locations and, as they are a fair distance apart, you realise that you must identify which is which. You could take a compass bearing along the line of the stream (as described in the next section) and then compare this with the direction of the two streams on the map. In this case, however, both streams appear to run in roughly the same direction, so it is far easier to orientate your map along the line of, first, one stream, and then the other. By comparing the topography with what is shown on the map, it should be a simple task to work out exactly which pool you are near.

Choose either of the possible pools on the map, then, using the stream as the linear feature, line everything up so that the stream you see on the map runs in the same direction as the stream you see on the ground. Now compare the topography with the contour patterns. You may find that the map shows the land sloping down to the left, whereas you can see that the land rises to the left. So you

Mountain pools can often be used to locate yourself in difficult terrain. However, in moorland areas, many lie just below the level of the surrounding moorland and can be extremely difficult to find. You should be aware that small pools may become dry in summer, or may even have disappeared since the map was published. Location = SO/152159. View approximately 032° Mag.

then line up the other pool and – hey presto!' – the map shows the land rising to the left. Any other features which you can see are also in the correct position. Would that it were always that simple! More often than not you will have to compare the land all around you until you reach any definite conclusion.

In the second example, you are about to descend into a valley after a good day's walking in an area which you have not visited before. As you begin the descent, and the view starts to open out, you see, to your horror, that the whole of one side of the valley is afforested. Your immediate thought is that you are descending into the wrong valley because your map gives no indication of any afforestation near your chosen route. While you realise that this could simply be due to the fact that your map is out of date, not only do you know that you have the latest map, you also see that there is another valley nearby which has a Forestry Commission plantation in an equivalent position.

Obviously, what you have to decide is whether you are descending into the correct valley which has been afforested since your map was printed, or whether you are descending, incorrectly, into the valley shown to be afforested on your map. It may well be that a single bearing (as described, yet again, in Part Three) will solve the problem, but you should be able to work things out simply by setting the map, using the line of the valley as the linear feature, and then comparing the topography with the contour patterns, etc.

Owing to the fact that no two areas of land are exactly the same, it is impossible to give hard and fast rules relating to the way you solve these types of problems. Personal preference will also play a part, and different people are likely to solve similar problems in totally different ways, even though their preferred methods are all based upon similar techniques. As was said at the start, knowledge of the basic techniques is not enough; you must gain practical experience so that you can apply a certain amount of reasoning to any problem with which you are faced.

When you are able to set and and interpret your map, you will find, increasingly, that you are able to predict what features lie ahead of you on your route. This is the beginning of accurate navigation. You know the scale of your map (you have a quick

Map interpretation will play a large part when navigating in terrain such as this. Study the contours carefully so that you get the 'feel' of the shape of your surroundings. Where there are no obvious features, you may have to follow a compass bearing, even in good visibility. Location = SO/128152. View approximately 027° Mag.

reference as to distance on any map because you know that the grid lines are always exactly 1 km apart), and by using this in conjunction with the contour lines and other conventional signs, you will be able to keep yourself on any chosen route more easily.

You may, for example, see from your map that in approximately 500 m you will pass a small lake to your left and then start to go uphill. If, after 500 m, you pass a small lake to your right and start to go downhill, you will know either that you are off route, or that your map reading could still do with some improvement. If, after 700 m, you have still seen no sign of a lake, even though the visibility is excellent, I would respectfully suggest that you should not have gone on to the hill in the first place.

In the next section you will be shown how to work out how many minutes it will take you to get to the lake, how many paces you will take on the way, and how you can get safely back to civilisation when the mist is so thick that you are unable to see the lake even when you are less than 5 m from it.

Before you progress any further, however, you *must* master the art of map interpretation. All the later-learned techniques rely on your ability to interpret a map, and are virtually useless unless you can do so. Eventually, you will start to see your map as a picture of the landscape rather than a mass of lines, symbols and colours.

To recap: map interpretation is the art of reading a map like a good novel. Instead of the conventional signs, contour lines and such like appearing as separate symbols, they are read in conjunction with one another to give you an accurate and vivid description of the terrain.

Following a linear feature such as a footpath is straightforward, but make sure you are on the correct path. In many areas, pony tracks and sheep tracks can look remarkably like little-used footpaths. This path crosses a stream (slightly right of centre). This stream crossing can be used to pinpoint your position along the path. Location = SH/601470. View approximately 035° Mag.

2.8 **Route planning and route finding**

Selecting a route is an important part of mountain navigation and hill-walking. Although, like many other things, it is best learned through experience, a few words on the subject at this stage will not go amiss.

For the purposes of this book, we are going to make a distinction between, on the one hand, route planning and, on the other, route finding. In many ways this distinction is arbitrary, for in practice you will find that the two go together. Both terms should be relatively self-explanatory.

Route planning is the general process of deciding roughly where to go on a walk (i.e. the overall plan). There are a number of points which should affect your final choice, including the size and fitness of the party, the type of terrain to be crossed, the time of year (mountain days are very short in the winter), whether you intend to camp on the hill (and will, therefore, be carrying a fair amount of weight). You should also take note of the weather forecast, and for this reason it is perhaps better not to make any definite plans until the night before you are due to go. Leaving it this late has the added advantage that everything will be fresh in your mind for, as you pore over the map working out your route, you will begin to get an idea of the general topography of the area.

Route finding is concerned with the precise route of each stage (or leg) of the walk, and can be defined as the art of selecting the easiest, or most suitable, route between two points. A common belief is that this route will always be a straight line, but this is rarely the case. In general, you should try to avoid walking directly between two points – except, as described later, in very misty conditions – as there is almost certain to be a far better alternative.

The easiest route is rarely the shortest. Indeed, it is often possible to tell the experience of a party (or of a party's leader) simply by watching the route they follow. On numerous occasions one can watch an inexperienced leader take his group directly from one point to another, involving them in toiling up one side of a short, steep spur and then dropping down on the other side. A more experienced leader would probably have led his group around the base of the spur, or taken a gently rising traverse line, instead of tackling it direct.

One of the 'rules' of mountaincraft is that you should try not to lose or gain any height unnecessarily. It is a waste of both time and energy to climb 100 m only to lose it again when there is a far easier, albeit slightly longer, alternative. Once you start walking in the high mountains, you will soon find that you have enough climbing to do without adding to it unnecessarily.

Another point worth mentioning is the danger of descending convex slopes, especially in conditions of poor visibility. Convex slopes are those which become steeper as they descend and, owing to their shape, it is often impossible to see what is below you. Any large cliff would obviously be shown on your map, but drops of less than 4 m are often not shown. 4 m is a long way to fall!

For similar reasons, it is inadvisable to descend gullies or stream beds. Your view of the surrounding countryside is likely to be restricted, wet and/or mossy rocks can be lethal in Vibram soles, and water always takes the line of least resistance (e.g. it likes to travel vertically downwards whenever it can). Even if you do not fall over the edge of a cliff, you may be faced with a vertical drop or an impassable section, and it may be impossible to climb out of the gully without retracing your steps for some distance. If you have had any difficulty on the way down, you can be certain you will have even more difficulty on the way back up.

To recap: route planning is simply deciding on where you are going for a day's walking, and can be done from the map. Route finding needs practice, and is the art of finding the easiest route between two points.

2.9 **Route cards**

It is a good idea to make out a *route card* before setting off into the hills. This can be used in a number of ways, not only as an aid to mountain safety, but also as a form of reference document which will be of great help in those situations where, owing to the weather conditions or some other problem, you need all the help you can get.

In its simplest form, a route card consists of a very brief description of your proposed route, together with a few details of the places you are going to visit or pass along the way. A more detailed route card would contain grid references, compass bearings, distances, estimated times, escape routes, specific comments or warnings about potential hazards, and a host of other information which you feel may be useful to you (or others) during your walk. However, it should be noted that at this early stage it is inadvisable for you to attempt any route which requires this amount of detail unless you are accompanied by someone with a fair degree of experience.

Route cards come in many different formats, and there are no hard and fast rules regarding how they should be laid out; it is purely a matter of personal preference. Nevertheless, for what should be fairly obvious reasons, it is essential that the information contained in them is clear both to you and to others. There should be no ambiguities. It is, therefore, a good idea to practise making out route cards whenever possible, certainly until you have a tried and tested format which can be easily understood by everyone.

The importance of clarity should not be underestimated. The route card is there not only to help you, but to help others find you should you get into difficulties. When you go into the mountains, you should make two copies of the card, and leave one with someone responsible, together with a note of the time at which you expect to return. In the event of an accident or some other mishap, a rescue team can be called out and, by following the details you have noted on the card, they should be able to find you more quickly than if they knew only the approximate area in which you

As you walk along an obvious path, there are often numerous ways in which to keep track of your position. In this picture the ruined miners' chapel is an obvious feature, and there are further ruins just before the path leaves the valley floor and curves around to climb gently up the side of the mountain. Even if there were no ruins, the bend in the track followed by the start of an ascent should be enough to give you your location. Location = SH/672463. View approximately 282° Mag.

were walking.

Route cards are, unfortunately, very controversial these days, because a large number of people insist that by using them they deny themselves the 'freedom of the hills', this being the main reason they went into the mountains in the first place. However, while I would be the last person to state emphatically that everyone should rigidly follow a route-card description each time they go into mountainous or hilly areas, I feel certain that most people would agree that you should always leave at least a few details of your approximate route with a responsible person, especially at the beginning of your hill-walking 'career'. If you do this, it is just as important to *let them know when you return*. Many's the time a mountain rescue team has been called out to look for an overdue party, only to find that they have descended safely and are enjoying themselves in some local hostelry, having neglected to tell anyone that they have returned. As you can imagine, members of rescue teams are somewhat annoyed when this occurs!

Writing a route card has other advantages which can make all the difference to a day's walking, especially if you are in an unfamiliar area. For a start, in order to compile one with any measure of accuracy, you will be forced to sit down and study your map before you go, thereby familiarising yourself with the basic shape of the area. While you are doing this, it is a good idea to work out some *escape routes* along which you can easily retreat should the weather turn against you, or something unforeseen occur. These should be easy-to-follow, straightforward routes leading down to the nearest valley or civilisation. Do not forget that, as with route finding, the easiest route will not necessarily be the quickest nor the most direct.

Ideally you are looking for an escape route along which it will be relatively simple to navigate, which gives you as much shelter from inclement conditions as possible, and down which it would be possible to carry an injured person. Knowledge of the terrain can play a large part here, and if you are less than about a third of the way through your walk, you may even find it easiest to retrace your steps. 'Text-book' escape routes very rarely occur in practice, but whatever lines you decide to take, choose them with care, and remember that if you are forced to use them, something will have gone wrong. You could be tired, wet and cold, and helping along an injured person. Details of your chosen escape routes should be given on *both* copies of your route card so that, if the worst comes to the worst, the rescue teams will know where to look in addition to your main route.

When you start using the techniques described in Part Three, you will find that route cards have definite advantages, for you can work out and note down compass bearings, time and distance estimations, etc. in comfort, before going on to the hill. It can be amazingly difficult trying to work out a compass bearing when your hands are cold, the rain is lashing into your eyes, and your map is slowly disintegrating because of gusts of wind, yet this is the very time when you need an accurate bearing! Your route card, carefully worked out the night before, can solve this problem.

A sample route card illustrating one type of layout is shown in Fig. 7. Note how the comments in the 'remarks' column can be used as a check that you are still on course, how particular features have been located by using grid references, and the way in which there are escape routes for various parts of the walk. Note also how each leg of the walk is kept relatively short, especially in difficult terrain. This is so that the deviation resulting from any error will be kept small. Any error which you make in navigation will obviously result in some form of deviation from your proper course. The further the distance of each leg, the greater will be the resultant deviation when you finally realise you are going wrong, and the greater the difficulty you will then have in relocating yourself. This is explained in more detail in the next section.

To recap: route cards, although controversial, are useful aids to navigation, especially when conditions are poor. To be of any use to you or others, they should give all the necessary information in a clear and unambiguous way.

2.10 The importance of practice

Map reading and interpretation are the keys to successful mountain

Front of card

30/5/85	STARTING FROM LAYBY ON B4560 (162160)					
FEATURE	GRID REF	M°	DIST METRES	HT ↑ FEET	TIME MINS	REMARKS
QUARRY	158162	-	600	50	9	Follow Road + Track
TRIG. POINT	147159	260	1175	175	20	Pool on left after 700 metres
POOL	137150	234	1350	-	16	Small outcrop + dry valley 2/3 along
POOL IN DEPRESSION	134150	277	300	25	5	Many similar Depressions beyond
POOL	139148	121	550	-	6	Cross FP after 350 metres
POOL	143143	145	600	-	7	Rocky ground FP @ 400 metres
POOL	157149	073	1500	25	19	Old working + boggy ground @ 600 metres
LAYBY	162160	033	1150	175	19	Aim off to road Steer 040° MAG.

M° = Magnetic bearing, HT. ↑ = Height climbed

Back of card

SIZE OF PARTY = 4 ADULTS	
ESTIMATED TIME OF RETURN = 1800 HRS	

ESCAPE ROUTES :-

① HEAD DUE EAST TO B4560

② HEAD TO LLANGYNIDR RESERVOIR (152141) THEN SE ALONG TRACK TO ROAD

Fig. 7. Sample route card. This route card describes a short, 'navigation practice' walk taken from Ordnance Survey 1:25,000 Outdoor Leisure Map, Abergavenny and the Black Mountains. Explanations of distances, timings and bearings will be found in Part Three.

The importance of practice

navigation. Once you have mastered the basic skills outlined so far, you will be ready to progress to the next stage, in which you will learn how to use a compass and to navigate accurately even when the visibility is so poor that you can hardly see the other members of your party, let alone any distinguishing features on the landscape.

No amount of theory will make you skilled at map interpretation – *you must gain practical experience*. Go into the hills as often as you can and practise your map work. Because you are bound to make some mistakes to begin with, do not be tempted to try anything too ambitious too soon. The more difficult expeditions can be left until you have mastered both map interpretation and the techniques described in Part Three.

In good weather you should be able to navigate using your map alone, but when conditions close in and the visibility becomes almost non-existent, life can become extremely harrowing. Navigation will start to require your total concentration, and the going can get rough. This is the time when you will need a few other techniques at your fingertips, for it is under these conditions that most accidents occur. One hears stories of benightment, exposure and falling over cliffs, but the cause of these and many other accidents can often be traced directly to an initial error of navigation.

By themselves, the techniques described in Part Three are useless. To be of any help to you they must be used in conjunction with a map, and to use them successfully and accurately you must be able to interpret that map.

Remember – the contents of Part Three are not alternatives to map interpretation but aids to it. You should only need to use them when conditions are such that you need pinpoint accuracy.

To recap: map reading and interpretation are the most important parts of mountain navigation. Without a good level of skill in map work you will not be accurate, even if you know all there is to know about the additional techniques described next. The only way to gain a high level of skill at map interpretation is through practice.

The map comes first – the compass comes second.

Part three
Additional techniques

3.1 Introduction

So far, we have been concentrating on the use of the map in order to lay a firm foundation for the growth of your skill at mountain navigation. In this part of the book we will go on to discuss a variety of other techniques which can be used as *aids* to map interpretation (*not* alternatives), especially in conditions of poor visibility.

Before doing this, however, it may be helpful to look in more detail at the mnemonic CROOK which was mentioned at the start of section 2.7. You will remember that the C stands for concentration, the R for reasoning, the two Os for observation and organisation and the K for knowledge. Let us now look at each of these key words in more detail.

Concentration is necessary when you need to pinpoint your position or follow a particular course in poor conditions. Undoubtedly, there will be times when other members of your party can help, especially if they are as experienced as – or more experienced than – you, but in general you should insist that your colleagues must not disturb your concentration when you are navigating, especially in a tricky or potentially dangerous situation.

Reasoning is necessary by virtue of the fact that the land is dynamic whereas your map is static. There is always the possibility that your map may be wrong, and it is important that you realise this, otherwise you may think you are lost when, in reality, you are not.

Reasoning is also important when it comes to route planning and route finding, and when things go wrong. More about this latter point later.

Observation is necessary at all times and, like map interpretation

More ways in which to pinpoint your position. Note the linear feature (the track), the intersection of another linear feature (the stream) and the ruins. Location = SH/678459. View approximately 277° Mag.

in general, it should be a two-way process. Not only should you be looking for features which you have seen on the map, you should also be watching the land around you and relating the information back on to the map as a check on your progress. On a clear day, for example, you may well be wandering along without any regular reference to your map. If the cloud suddenly comes down (and it can appear with amazing speed), you will have great difficulty in working out your position unless you have been observant. If you know your general direction (which you can find out by observation), and you remember that you saw (or passed) some feature or other about 5 minutes before, you immediately have a fair estimate of where you are.

Organisation is necessary if you are to make any sense of the mass of data which you should be getting through concentration, reasoning and observation. It also helps to make life more pleasant when something has gone wrong or the weather has closed in unexpectedly. You should be organised right from the word go. Your map should be folded in such a way that you can refer to it immediately. Your compass should be easily accessible without the need to unpack your rucksack. You should have browsed over the map the night before and made notes (i.e. a route card) which will help you if the going gets rough.

Always try to work to a definite plan when it comes to poor visibility navigation. There are so many little things you can do to make your navigation easier and more effective. All this organisation may sound like the very thing you came to the mountains to avoid, but having some form of system to which you can work, even if it is simply a matter of tackling each leg of navigation in a systematic way, will almost certainly increase the enjoyment you get from being in the mountains.

Knowledge is necessary for obvious reasons, but it does not simply refer to a knowledge of the techniques of mountain navigation. You should also know which techniques to use in what situation, and this knowledge should be so firmly ingrained that you feel no need to hesitate before putting it into practice. This is especially important if you are leading a group, for any dithering on the part of the leader, especially in poor conditions, is going to have a disastrous effect on group morale.

It goes without saying that a knowledge of the area in which you are walking would be of great help. Even if you are visiting a particular area for the first time, you will be able to pick up a vast amount of useful information when you pore over the map to plan your route the night before.

3.2 The compass

Compasses come in a huge variety of different shapes and sizes, some of which have been designed for specialist applications and are, therefore, not particularly suitable for use in the mountains. The range extends from the old fashioned 'boy-scout' compass (useful for getting a rough idea of direction, but little else) to incredibly expensive and heavy 'prismatic' or 'optical sighting' compasses which can be read to within a quarter of a degree. Both types do the job for which they were designed, but are of limited use when walking in the mountains (see also Appendix IV). A good compass for mountain navigation should be able to do far more than simply find north!

By far the best and most commonly used models for mountain work are those manufactured by Silva. These are known as 'protractor-compasses' or 'orienteering compasses' and, although a number of similarly designed instruments have appeared on the market in recent years, there is little doubt that Silva is still the brand leader.

The type of compass best suited to our purposes really consists of two separate parts: the compass housing, which contains the magnetic needle, and the base plate, which is used, amongst other things, as a protractor. A typical compass of this type is shown in Fig. 8.

The *compass housing* (1) is a circular plastic container, usually filled with a clear oil, inside which pivots the magnetic *needle* (2), one half of which is white, the other half being red. The red end of the compass is often referred to as the *north seeking end*, for it will point towards magnetic north – assuming you are using your compass correctly! The top rim of the compass housing is divided into 180 numbered segments, each segment representing 2° of arc, and the relative positions of north, south, east and west are marked. On the transparent base of the housing are a number of fine, parallel lines known as the *orienting lines* (3), the central two of which are joined to form an arrow – the *orienting arrow* (4).

The whole housing is surrounded by a collar, and this collar is attached to the rest of the compass in such a way that the housing can be turned through 360°. This movement should be smooth but reasonably firm. Any sticking or jerkiness will make it difficult for you to set bearings accurately, and if the housing turns too freely there is always the danger that you may inadvertently alter the setting.

The *base plate* or *protractor* (5) usually contains a magnifying *lens* (6) to aid map interpretation, and has one or more *scales* in centimetres and/or inches printed along the front and the sides (7). Now that the vast majority of maps have been metricated, you will find the centimetre scales the most useful. Some models have an

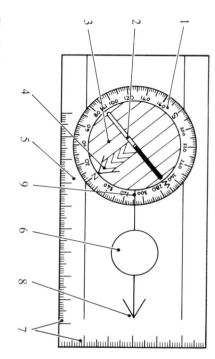

Fig. 8. The protractor-compass.

extra set of scales called *Romer scales*, the function of which will be described later.

The base plate also has three or more fine, parallel lines running along its length. These are also parallel to the sides of the base plate, and the centre line has a large arrow – the *direction of travel arrow* – at its front end (8). This same centre line also runs back to the compass housing where it is visible under the numbered segments (9). It is at this point that you read off your bearings.

As was said at the beginning of this section, a good compass for mountain navigation should have a number of uses. The type described above fits the bill perfectly. Apart from finding north (by itself, not very useful), it can be used to work out accurate grid references and distances, to set the map in poor visibility, and to work out bearings both from the map and from the ground. It will also enable you to follow these bearings with a high degree of accuracy.

You already know how to give a grid reference correct to at least six figures, and you will, I hope, remember that a six-figure reference covers an area 100 m square (i.e. a total area of 10,000 m²). Having a scale printed on your compass base plate enables you to be more accurate whenever necessary. Instead of having to estimate the tenths of a square, you can now measure them exactly. Likewise, you can also measure distances instead of estimating them (see also section 3.5 – Estimating distance).

To recap: While there are many different types of compass on the market, it is the protractor-compass or orienteering compass which is the most useful for mountain navigation. In addition to giving you general direction, this can be used to work out and follow accurate bearings both from the map and from the ground, to facilitate the calculation of grid references and distances, etc.

3.3 Bearings

The most important use of your compass is in the taking, setting and following of bearings. These can be used not only to give you an

accurate direction of travel in poor visibility, but also as a means of pinpointing your position. Some people may find the procedures a little confusing or complex to begin with, but (as with the rest of mountain navigation) once you have mastered the basic principles you should find using bearings very simple. Let us first look at the way in which you can work out your direction of travel.

We said earlier that the base plate of the compass is also known as the protractor. A protractor is simply a device for measuring angles (exactly the same as the protractors in geometry sets), and *bearings* are simply angles measured with respect to north. Convention has it that all bearings in mountain navigation are quoted in 'degrees east of north'; in other words, you always measure the angle in a clockwise direction. Thus, looking at the *cardinal points* (i.e. north, east, south and west), north is 0°, east is 90°, south is 180° and west is 270°. This is shown quite clearly in Fig. 9.

Let us assume that you are standing at point A, and you wish to travel to point B which may well be out of sight owing to poor visibility or any number of other reasons. In order to calculate the bearing, you must measure the angle between a line from point A (your present position) to point B (your destination) and another line between point A and north, as shown clearly in Fig. 10.

The first thing you must do is find the positions of both point A and point B on the map. You must be accurate when you do this. It is not enough to find their approximate positions; you must find their *exact* locations. Once you have done this, place your compass on the map in such a way that one side of the base plate (or one of the parallel lines on the base plate) runs precisely between the two points, and the direction of travel arrow points in the direction in which you wish to travel (in this case, from A to B). The compass should now be in such a position that, were you to run a pencil along the side of the base plate, the resulting straight line would join

If needs be, you could take a compass bearing along the line of the path, then compare this with the map, in order to work out your approximate position. To be more exact you could use the obvious bend on the path (or its associated rock buttress) to pinpoint your position. (See also page 87.) Location = SO/196159. View approximately 237° Mag.

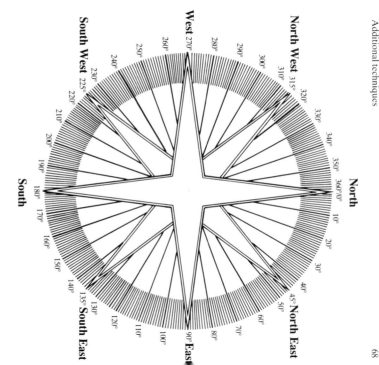

Fig. 9. Cardinal points.

points A and B (or would run parallel to an imaginary straight line joining the two points). This is shown in the upper part of Fig. 11.

Ignoring the compass needle for the moment, and keeping the base plate firmly and accurately in position between the two points, turn the compass housing until the orienting lines are exactly parallel to the north-south grid lines, and the orienting arrow is pointing to the northern (top) edge of the map. This position is

Bearings

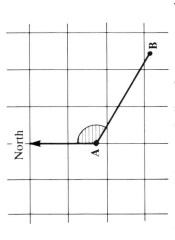

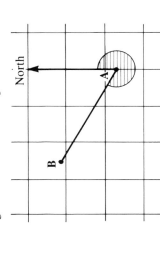

A bearing is the angle between the line of your course and north. This is always measured in degrees east of north (i.e. in a clockwise direction from north).

In both these diagrams your course will take you from A to B, and your bearing is therefore the angle that line A-B makes with a north-south grid line, measured in degrees east of that line.

The angle measured to determine the bearing is shown by the shaded area. Point A is situated on a grid line purely for convenience; in practice it can lie anywhere in the grid square. The method by which you measure bearings with your compass is shown in Fig. 11.

Fig. 10. Bearings.

Top (northern edge) of map

Place the compass on the map so that one side of the base plate touches both points (A and B), and the direction of travel arrow points in the direction in which you wish to go. Ignore the compass needle.

Without moving the base plate, turn the compass housing until the orienting lines lie parallel to the north-south grid lines, and the orienting arrow points towards the northern edge of the map. Now read off the figure at the back of the direction of travel arrow.

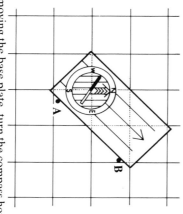

Fig. 11. Calculating bearings from the map.

shown in the lower part of Fig. 11. Now read off the figure where the direction of travel arrow intersects the numbered segments on the compass housing, not forgetting that each segment represents 2° You should be accurate to within 1°. The figure you now have is known as a *grid bearing*.

So far, so good – but we now come to a slight complication. The problem is that the figure shown on your compass represents the value of an angle taken with respect to grid north (the north to which the grid lines on your map are pointing). Unfortunately, the needle on your compass does not point to grid north, but to magnetic north, which is in a totally different place! The difference in angle between these two norths is known as the *magnetic variation* and, owing to the nature of the earth's magnetic field and the fact that the position of the magnetic pole (i.e. magnetic north) tends to 'wobble about', this magnetic variation alters slightly from place to place and from year to year, as mentioned in Part One. In Britain, the current magnetic variation (1986) is between 6° and 8° west of grid north, depending on which part of the country you happen to be in.

All Ordnance Survey maps have the magnetic variation for that area printed in the key, together with the rate of annual change. Although this rate of change is very small, you should always check it and adjust the magnetic variation accordingly. For example, you may find written: 'Magnetic north approximately 8° west of grid north in 1975, decreasing by about 0.5° in four years.' The magnetic variation for that particular area in 1986 would therefore be approximately 7°.

The procedure by which you change your grid bearing into a usable *magnetic bearing* is very straightforward; all you need to do is *add* the magnetic variation as illustrated in Fig. 12. If you have a grid bearing of 126° and the magnetic variation is 7°W, your magnetic bearing will be 133°. So long as the magnetic variation is west of grid north – and it will be, in this country, for some time to come – adding the magnetic variation to a grid bearing will always give you the corresponding magnetic bearing. The easiest way to do this on your compass is to turn the housing in an anticlockwise direction until the required number of degrees have been added,

The size of the magnetic variation differs from area to area, but is always indicated in the key of every Ordnance Survey map. There will also be a reference to 'true north'; you need not worry about this as it will not concern you when navigating in the hills.

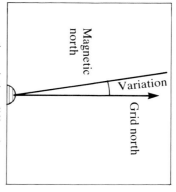

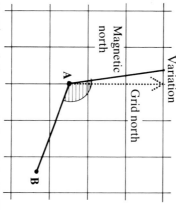

When the magnetic variation is west of north (as it will be in the British Isles for many years to come), you always **add** the amount of variation in degrees to your grid bearing in order to calculate your magnetic bearing. The diagram should make the reason for this quite clear.

Fig. 12. Magnetic variation.

remembering that each segment represents 2°. It is a good idea also to do the calculation in your head as an added check. Some of your magnetic bearings can obviously be worked out the night before a walk and noted on your route card.

Once you have arrived at the magnetic bearing, you can find out the exact direction in which you must travel to get from your present position at point A to your destination at point B. Up to this stage, you have been using your compass as a protractor and should, therefore, have been ignoring the compass needle. You are now going to use it to find a specific direction – this direction being the bearing which you have just calculated – and you should now take note of the compass needle and ignore the fact that the housing moves. Obviously, you can set any bearing you want simply by turning the housing so that the required figure is shown. What this means is that if you accidentally turn the housing while you are following a particular bearing, you are effectively altering the bearing, and will therefore end up in totally the wrong place!

Hold the compass in front of you, with the direction of travel arrow pointing directly away from you. *Without moving the compass housing* slowly turn around until the *red* end of the needle lies exactly over the orienting arrow. The direction of travel arrow will now be pointing exactly to point B. Simple, isn't it? The method by which you follow this bearing is described in the next section, but first let us look at some of the other uses to which bearings can be put.

Earlier in the book, we described the technique of setting the map by map interpretation. It is often extremely useful to set the map in conditions of poor visibility or on other occasions when there are no definite features to which you can refer. In these situations, you can set the map using your compass.

Place the map on a flattish surface, then lay the compass on top in such a way that the edge of the base plate lies parallel to the north–south grid lines, and the direction of travel arrow points towards the northern (top) edge of the map. The compass housing should be turned to show a bearing of due north (i.e. 0°). At this setting, the orienting arrow will be in line with the direction of travel arrow, and the orienting lines in the base of the housing will be parallel to the edges of the base plate. Now turn the map and compass together, keeping the edge of the base plate exactly parallel with the north–south grid lines, until the *red* end of the needle lies directly over the orienting arrow. Your map will now be set for most practical purposes, but if you wish to be really accurate, you must take the magnetic variation into consideration.

By far the easiest way to compensate for the magnetic variation in this situation is simply to set the compass to the value of the magnetic variation. In other words, if the magnetic variation is 7°W, you should set your compass to 7° instead of 0°. All you are doing is following the same procedure as when you change a grid bearing to a magnetic bearing – adding the variation. When you have set the variation on your compass, simply follow exactly the same procedure as before, lining up the sides of the base plate with the north–south grid lines, making sure that the direction of travel arrow points towards the northern edge of the map, then turning both map and compass together until the *red* end of the needle lies directly over the orienting arrow (see Fig. 13).

Another technique which can be extremely useful in certain situations is that of being able to check your position quickly and accurately. This can be done by taking a bearing on some feature which you can both see on the ground and identify on the map. To do this, hold the compass in front of you with the direction of travel arrow pointing directly at your chosen feature. You will be far more accurate if you hold the compass just below eye level and sight along the line between the pivot of the needle and the end of the direction of travel arrow. Keeping this arrow accurately lined up with the feature, turn the compass housing until the *red* end of the needle lies directly over the direction of travel arrow. The figure shown where the end of the direction of travel arrow intersects the edge of the compass housing is the magnetic bearing from you to the chosen feature.

This technique does require a fair amount of practice, for the position in which you hold your compass is extremely important in terms of the degree of accuracy. At best, this position is a compromise between being able to sight directly along the direction of travel arrow, and being able to look directly down on to the

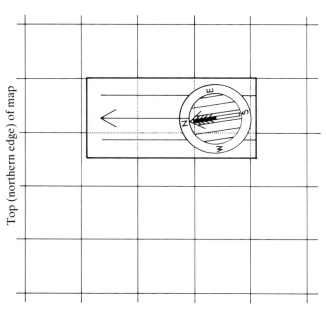

Top (northern edge) of map

Fig. 13. Setting the map with a compass.

Stage one. Set the compass to show due north (0° or 360°) **or**, if you wish to be really accurate, set it to the magnetic variation (as shown in this diagram).

Stage two. Place the compass on the map so that one side of the base plate lies along a north-south grid line, and the direction of travel arrow points toward the northern edge of the map.

Stage three. Keeping the edge of the base plate in line with the grid lines, turn the whole map until the red (north-seeking) end of the compass needle lies directly over the orienting arrow. The map will now be set in the correct orientation.

needle and orienting arrow. Although you might find the sighting quite difficult to begin with, once you gain experience you should be able to take bearings in this manner correct to within 1°. (See also Appendix IV – The optical sighting compass.)

To use your magnetic bearing in order to check your position on the map, you must first convert it to a grid bearing. What you have done on this occasion is measure the angle between a line from you to the feature and a line from you to magnetic north. As we have seen, magnetic north and grid north are different, so before you can use this bearing on your map, you must take into account the magnetic variation. The rule, exactly as mentioned earlier, is quite straightforward. Any bearing taken with a compass is a magnetic bearing, and must be converted before it can be used on the map. Any bearing taken from the map is a grid bearing, and must be converted before it can be used with a compass.

To convert your magnetic bearing to a grid bearing you simply *subtract* the magnetic variation, the reason for this being shown in Fig. 12.

Whenever the magnetic variation is west of grid north (and it will be everywhere in the British Isles for some time) you can always convert bearings by using the following rule:

> Convert *grid* bearings to *magnetic* bearings by *adding* the magnetic variation.
> Convert *magnetic* bearings to *grid* bearings by *subtracting* the magnetic variation.

Once the necessary conversion has been made and you have altered the setting of your compass to the converted figure, you will be in a position to use the grid bearing to find out where you are. Place the compass on the map with the front end of one side of the base plate resting against the feature whose bearing you have just taken. You are now going to use the compass as a protractor, so you should ignore the needle. Turn the base plate (or the map) until the orienting lines in the compass housing line up with the north–south grid lines, and the orienting arrow points towards the northern edge of the map. The front end of one side of the base plate should still,

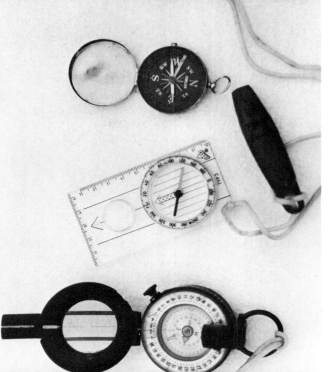

Various types of compass. From left to right: MOD prismatic compass. Silva protractor-compass, 'boy-scout' type compass.

obviously, lie against the feature. If this same edge also lies against the position at which you think you are standing, then you are most probably correct. What can be said with certainty, however, all other things being equal, is that you are standing somewhere along the line formed by the edge of the base plate.

Let us assume that you are not really sure where you are. You see an obvious feature which you can identify on the map, and so you take a bearing as described above. After doing the necessary conversion, you lay the compass on the map and line up the orienting lines with the north–south grid lines, always checking, of

Top (northern edge) of map

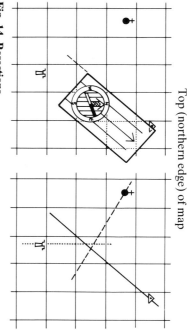

Fig. 14. Resections.

Stage one. Sight along the compass and take a bearing on an object or feature which you can readily identify both on the ground and on the map. Convert this magnetic bearing to a grid bearing by **subtracting** the magnetic variation.

Stage two. Place the compass on the map in such a way that the front of one side of the base plate lies against the object on which you took the bearing. Turn the base plate (**not** the housing) until the orienting lines are parallel to the north-south grid lines, and the orienting arrow points towards the northern edge of the map.

Stage three. Draw a line along the side of the base plate which lies against the object on which the bearing was taken. Your position is somewhere along that line.

Stage four. Up to two further lines can be drawn if necessary, using the same method. Ideally, each new bearing should be approximately 120° away from the last. After having drawn three lines, you will most likely end up with a small triangle where the three lines intersect. Your position will be in the centre of this triangle.

course, that the orienting arrow is pointing in the right direction. As soon as you have done this, you have narrowed down your possible position to a thin line, and it may often be possible to confirm or pinpoint your position simply by map interpretation. If, for example, you are standing at (or close to) a linear feature, such as a sharp ridge, a river, a long field boundary or a path, your position will be at (or near) the point where the edge of the base plate crosses that feature on the map. If you want to make certain of your position, especially if you are nowhere near any linear feature, you can do a *resection* as described below and in Fig. 14. However, even though resections are fairly simple, they are rarely used in mountain navigation for two main reasons. Firstly, it is rare for the visibility to be good enough to enable you successfully to take a resection in those situations where you feel there is a need; and secondly, if the visibility is good enough, it should be good enough for you to be able to pinpoint your position by map interpretation alone!

You have already done the first stage of a resection by taking a bearing on an object as described above. While the compass is in the correct position on the map, draw a line from the feature, along the side of the base plate, and into the area in which you think you are standing. Now take a second bearing on another feature, preferably about 120° away from the first. Treat this bearing in exactly the same way as the first and draw a second line on the map. This second line should cross the first, and the point at which they cross will be your position, the accuracy of this point depending upon the accuracy of your compass work. If your life depends on your knowing exactly where you are, take a third bearing, preferably a further 120° away, and draw a third line. You will most probably find that you have formed a small triangle where the three lines meet, and your position should be somewhere inside that triangle. Unless you have been exceptionally accurate with all three bearings, there is no way that all three lines will meet at the same point.

While it is useful for you to know how to work out a resection, you will find that its use in mountain navigation is limited for the reasons outlined above. Indeed, one of the best uses for it is to give yourself a check on the accuracy of your compass work when you know where you are!

The technique of taking a bearing on an obvious feature can also be used to find the position of a change of course in those areas where, owing to the nature of the terrain, there are no suitable features to mark the spot. If, for example, you are walking along a ridge-top and wish to strike off at a particular point, you can work out the bearing of a distant object from that point on the map, then use your compass to confirm when you are in the correct position. This technique can obviously be used whenever you are following a linear feature (see Fig. 15).

One final technique which can be put to good use in a variety of situations is that of taking *back bearings* (see Fig. 16). Let us assume that you are walking along a bearing (as described in the next section) when you notice that the mist is starting to close in, or that you are just about to lose sight of the point from which you started this particular leg of the walk. If you turn around and sight along the direction of travel arrow so that it is pointing directly to your starting point, you should find that the *white* (southern) end of the compass needle lies directly over the orienting arrow. If it does, you are on the correct course. If it does not, you should move to the right or left until it does, at which time you will be back on course again.

So far, all the techniques have been described in isolation whereas, in reality, they are more usually combined. Once you have become familiar with them and, most importantly, gained practical experience of their use in a mountain environment, you will undoubtedly find ways of using them, either separately or in conjunction with one another, which have not been mentioned in this book. To be really successful at mountain navigation, not only do you need to have many different techniques at your fingertips, you should also know how and when to combine them to give you the best results. You should also never forget that all this compass work, and all the other techniques which are described later, should only be seen as additional, or subservient, to the basic mountain navigation skill – map interpretation.

There are two last points which must be stressed. Firstly, never forget that your compass needle is a magnet and will therefore be attracted to all metal objects and affected by all sources of

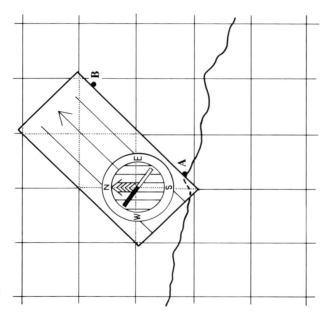

Fig. 15. Location on a linear feature. When standing at an unknown point on a linear feature, take a bearing on some object which you can both see and identify on the map.
Convert this to a grid bearing, then place the compass on the map with the front of one side of the base plate lying against this feature (B). Turn the base plate (**not** the housing) until the orienting lines lie parallel to the north-south grid lines and the orienting arrow points towards the northern edge of the map. You will be standing where the same edge of the base plate intersects the linear feature (A).

Back bearing. Note how the **white** (southern) end of the compass needle lies directly over the orienting arrow while the direction of travel arrow points to the position from which you have travelled (point A).

Standard bearing. Note how the **red** (north-seeking) end of the compass needle lies directly over the orienting arrow whilst the direction of travel arrow points towards the position for which you are making.

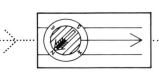 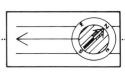

Fig. 16. Back bearings.

magnetism. When taking and using magnetic bearings, *keep the compass away from all metal objects.*

Some photographic exposure metres contain powerful magnets, so beware! It seems amazing how so many otherwise skilled mountain navigators forget this one simple point. One can almost guarantee that, at some time during your walking life, you will see someone using a compass while leaning against a wire fence or metal gate, or standing underneath electricity cables (which create an electro-magnetic field). To be on the safe side, keep your compass well away from anything which is made from, or might contain, metallic or magnetic material, including metal watch straps and electronic watches.

Because your compass needle is balanced on a pivot, you should also ensure that you use it in as horizontal a position as possible, and always give the needle time to settle down into the correct position before using a magnetic bearing. You are bound to be inaccurate if you use your compass while the needle is still swinging about, however gently.

Secondly, your compass invariably has a far better sense of direction than you. *Always trust your compass.*

The only exception to this is where there are magnetic rocks around (such as in the Black Cuillins of Skye), or something which causes a localised magnetic anomaly. Where these occur, they are normally well documented and should, in any event, be mentioned somewhere on the map. Obviously, you should be using your compass in the correct way, keeping it horizontal and well away from any magnetic or metallic objects.

To recap: bearings are simply angles. If you walk along a bearing of 45°, you are following a line which is at an angle of 45° to another line stretching from you to magnetic north. Because bearings taken from the map are grid bearings which use grid north as a reference point, you must always change them to magnetic bearings before following them on the ground. This is done simply by *adding* the magnetic variation (assuming that this variation is west, as it will be in this country for many years to come).

Not only can you use bearings to walk from one point to another,

The correct way to hold a protractor-compass. Note how the position is a compromise between able to sight directly along the direction of travel arrow, and being able to look directly down on the needle and orienting arrow.

you can also use them to pinpoint your position (with resections) and to check your course (with back bearings).

3.4 Walking on a bearing

Many people, when using a bearing for the first time, walk along desperately trying to keep the compass needle in the correct position over the orienting arrow while following the direction indicated by the direction of travel arrow. Invariably, because they are concentrating on the compass instead of looking where they are going, they fall over! This is obviously not the way to do it. Apart from leaving you with numerous bruises, it is also too much like hard work, and prevents you from looking around and enjoying the scenery. When used correctly, your compass will make walking along a bearing simplicity itself.

Once you have worked out your magnetic bearing and checked that it is indicated correctly on the rim of the compass housing, hold the compass in front of you with the direction of travel arrow pointing away from you, then turn round until the red end of the needle is lying directly over the orienting arrow (all as described at the beginning of the last section). Now get the compass into a position whereby you can sight along the direction of travel arrow yet still keep the red end of the needle accurately above the orienting arrow. What you need to find is some obvious feature, such as an isolated tree or an oddly shaped rock, which lies directly in line with the direction of travel arrow.

It is of paramount importance that this feature is something you can easily recognise. It is inadvisable, certainly to begin with, to choose a tree in a wood, or a boulder on a scree slope. Make sure, also, that it will not move. There is a story of a walker who took a sighting on a sheep in the mist and then proceeded to walk in a graceful arc as the creature took umbrage at his approach. Later on, with more experience and a great deal of concentration, you may find yourself in a position where you have to sight, literally, on a tussock of grass or even a ripple in the snow.

Once you have found a suitable, recognisable and static feature which lies directly on your direction of travel, you can dispense with your compass and simply walk to that feature. Once there, you repeat the procedure, and so on until you reach the destination of that particular leg of your walk. You should try to keep the distance between each object fairly short, ideally never more than about 50 m. The greater the distance, the greater will be any resulting error.

One of the greatest advantages of this method is that you are not forced to walk in a straight line, concentrating on your compass all the while. Once you have identified your objective, you can walk to it via the easiest or most interesting route. When ascending a steep slope, for example, it is far easier to zig-zag than to approach it direct. You can also by-pass obstacles such as mountain pools or particularly evil-looking bogs and, when faced with a wide stream, you can wander along the banks until you find a suitable crossing point. It does not matter where you go or how you get there, so long as you eventually reach the feature on which you sighted. This is another reason why this feature should be chosen with care, for you may eventually approach it from a slightly different direction. When following bearings in suitable conditions, feel free to wander about and enjoy yourself. 'Straight line' navigation has many obvious disadvantages, although sometimes one is forced to use it, as will be seen later.

This is all very well, and comparatively simple, in clear weather (when, incidentally, you should not usually need to follow a bearing because of your skills at map interpretation!) but in conditions of poor visibility it can be quite another story. If the conditions allow, you may well be able to sight on obvious features within your range of vision and carry on as before. To be safe, there are a number of other techniques which can be used to aid your progress. Once again, these additional techniques require practice and experience, perhaps even more so than anything which has gone before. You cannot hope to be accurate through theory alone.

This photograph is taken at the obvious bend in the track shown on page 66. In addition to the bend and rock buttress, you could confirm your position by taking a compass bearing on the obvious crag edge in the far distance. Location = SO/193156. View approximately 320° Mag.

To recap: The simplest way to follow a bearing is to use your compass to sight on a prominent object which lies directly on your course, and then to walk to it. This procedure is then repeated until you arrive at your destination.

3.5 **Estimating distance**

The estimation of distance plays an important part in accurate, poor visibility navigation. Like many other parts of mountain navigation it is a two-way process: not only is it helpful to know how far you have to travel between one objective and the next, it is also extremely useful if you can estimate, more or less exactly, how far you have travelled during any particular leg of navigation.

So far as estimating distance from the map is concerned, the procedure is simple. You know that the grid lines on all the Ordnance Survey maps you are likely to be using are exactly 1 km apart, and this will give you a rough guide. However, you really need to be far more precise, and this is where the scales on your compass base plate become useful.

Most compasses will have a scale (or scales) in centimetres and inches, or centimetres alone, printed along the sides and front of the base plate, as described in section 3.1. Some of the more expensive models also include a special set of scales known as *Romer scales*, the use of which is described below. As was mentioned earlier, now that most maps have been metricated you will find the centimetre and Romer scales the most useful.

On 1:50,000 scale maps, 1 cm on the map is equal to 50,000 cm (or 500 m) on the ground. Thus 1 mm equals 50 m. On 1:25,000 scale maps, by a similar calculation, 1 mm is equal to 25 m. If, to begin with, you are uncertain as to the values of the different scales, knock off the three final zeros from the scale ratio to give you the number of metres per millimetre (i.e. 1:25,000 becomes 1:25; 1 mm is equal to 25 m).

By using the scales on your compass base plate and measuring the distance between your present position and your objective, you should be able to obtain a fairly precise figure for the length of any leg of your walk. Obviously, this will be most accurate when you are walking in a straight line. However, this is just as well, for the time when you need to be accurate is when you are forced by the conditions or visibility to use almost strict, straight line navigation.

Counting up millimetres and doing even simple mental arithmetic in rough weather is no joke! Mistakes are easy to make, and you will need to concentrate. If your compass has a Romer scale your task will be less of a burden because Romer scales are those in which the conversion from millimetres to metres is done for you. Standard Romer scales are 1:63,360 (for the old One Inch series maps), 1:50,000 and 1:25,000, and all three are often to be found on the same base plate. Instead of reading off the distance in millimetres and then making the conversion, you simply read off the distance in metres. If your compass does not have this facility, it is well worth making your own Romer along the lines shown in Fig. 17. Because these scales work on the principle of dividing grid squares into tenths, they can also be used as a means of giving quick and accurate grid references.

It is not much use working out the precise length of a particular leg of navigation from the map unless you can put this information to good use on the ground. It may well be that you can judge roughly when you have walked 1 km across flat and even ground in fine weather, but in the mountains, when you can see less than 10 m in any direction and the wind is trying to blow you off your feet, 'roughly' is not good enough. In any case, unless you have some definite point of reference, travelling 100 m in a storm can feel like covering a distance of 1 km in fine conditions. It is when the going gets rough that the technique of *pacing* comes into its own.

Try to find a measured length of exactly 100 m. Admittedly, this can be difficult, but a good place to try is the local sports centre or athletic track. Alternatively, if you can get hold of a 100 m tape, measure the distance for yourself. If all these possibilities fail, go out with someone who can already use the technique accurately, and let them pace out the distance for you.

Using your normal stride and starting off with your right foot, walk the entire distance counting one pace every time your left foot touches the ground. It is best to do this at least three or four times.

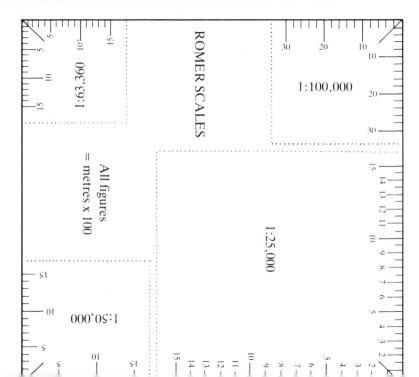

Fig. 17. The Romer scale. For explanation, see text.

Even in terrain apparently devoid of any definite features, it is often possible to confirm your position. Here the outcrop (slightly right of centre) and the shallow, dry valley (left of centre) can be used in combination. Location = SO/139152. View approximately 007° Mag.

Make a note of the total number of paces per 100 m. Once you have this information, it can be put to good use on the hill. If, for example, you take 65 paces per 100 m, and your next leg of navigation is 400 m in length, you know that you should arrive at the objective after 260 paces. However, you will obviously have to take into account a variety of other factors, such as the terrain, your physical fitness, whether you are carrying a heavy load or whether the wind is blowing directly against you, all of which are going to affect your length of stride. For example, on steep or very rough ground you will invariably take shorter strides than usual; on smooth, shallow downsloping ground the length of each stride is likely to increase. The amount of adjustment that is needed in different circumstances obviously varies from person to person, just as the original number of paces will vary, and your personal amounts of variation can only be found through experience.

Some people count every pace instead of counting 'double paces' as described above. The 'double pace' method is to be preferred as it involves smaller numbers. Step counting can be tedious at the best of times, and it is all too easy to lose count if your concentration is disturbed. Most people find that the easiest method is to count in 100 m steps, starting again from zero at the start of each succeeding 100 m. On longer legs, it is a good idea to have some means by which you can remember how many hundred metres you have counted. You can purchase a small device called a tachometer which fits on to the side of your compass base plate, and with which you can record how many hundreds of metres you have travelled. Simpler (and cheaper) is to use a handful of coins or pebbles. All you have to do after each 100 m is put a pebble in your pocket, or transfer a pebble from one hand to another. Make sure you remember which hand is which! These are only suggestions: you should find a method with which you feel happy and confident.

All this is not to imply that you should count paces all the time, every time you go on to the hills. In exactly the same way as you should not have to rely on your compass in good conditions, all the techniques described in this section are secondary to your map interpretation skills. You should only need to use these techniques in poor conditions or when you are in featureless terrain. However, because they all demand practice if you are to be at all accurate, it is a good idea to use them in good conditions until you become proficient, and to keep practising them every now and then, just to keep your hand in.

To recap: estimating distances can be a very useful technique, especially in conditions of poor visibility. Not only should you be able to estimate distances from the map, you should also be able to estimate distance covered on the ground. This is best done through step counting.

3.6 Estimating time

It is very useful to be able to estimate the duration of walks (or legs of walks) when in the hills. We all do it (or should do it) to a certain extent when we plan our walks. Estimating to the nearest hour, however, is not much help in those circumstances where accuracy is called for. Ideally, you should be able to estimate the duration of any leg of your walk to within a minute!

There is a formula, known as *Naismith's Rule*, which can be used as the basis for all estimations of time and duration. The original rule stated that, in the mountains, the 'average' person walked at 3 **miles per hour** and took an additional 30 minutes for each 1000 ft of ascent. The more useful metric equivalent is: *5 km per hour plus 30 minutes per 300 m of ascent.*

This is useful as a general guide so long as you remember to take every metre of ascent and descent into consideration. On one leg of a walk you may climb for 100 m, descend for 50 m, then climb again for a further 150 m. Although you have only gained 200 m of height, you have actually climbed 250 m, and it is this full amount which must be taken into consideration when using Naismith's Rule to estimate time. This is shown clearly in Fig. 18.

Quoted as above, Naismith's Rule is rather unwieldy, and you will find it far more simple to use if you break it down into smaller, more manageable units as below.

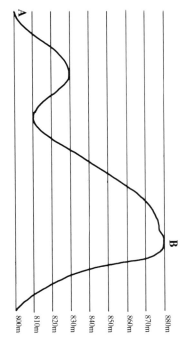

Fig. 18. Using Naismith's Rule. When travelling from A to B, although the height gained is only 80 m, the actual height climbed is 100 m. It is this full amount which must be taken into consideration when calculating times from Naismith's Rule.

5 km per hour = 12 minutes per kilometre
= 6 minutes per 500 m
= 1.2 minutes per 100 m
300 m per 30 minutes = 1 minute per 10 m of ascent

Regarding the amount of time which should be added for ascent, the contour lines on the Ordnance Survey Second Series 1:50,000 scale maps (i.e. the totally metricated series) have a vertical interval of 10 m. You can therefore simply add 1 minute extra for every contour line crossed when going uphill! The same applies to the totally metricated 1:25,000 scale maps in mountain areas, as the vertical interval is also 10 m. However, in lowland areas, the vertical interval on the new 1:25,000 scale maps is 5 m, so it is extremely important that you check the key in order to find out the size of the vertical interval.

Many of you will still be using maps in which the vertical interval is given in feet. This applies in particular to the Ordnance Survey

1:25,000 scale Outdoor Leisure Maps and the First Series 1:50,000 scale maps. Be especially careful when using the First Series 1:50,000 scale maps for, although the heights are quoted in metres, the vertical interval is given in feet. This is one of the temporary disadvantages we have to allow for while the Ordnance Survey finish their metrication programme. If you are using a map in which the vertical interval is quoted in feet, allow 3 minutes extra for every 100 ft of ascent. On the 1:25,000 scale maps, this corresponds to the darker contour lines, or 'index contours'.

Your speed over the ground will be affected by a number of variable factors, including your fitness (and the fitness of the rest of your party), the nature of the terrain, weather conditions, weight of rucksack, and any long, steep ascents or descents. What you must bear in mind is that Naismith's Rule is only meant to be a *guide* to the time you will take, not a hard and fast rule. Your estimate must therefore be adjusted with respect to the conditions at the time. There are a number of mind-boggling formulae (of which Tranter's Variations are probably the most widely known) which have been calculated especially so that you can make some of the necessary adjustments mathematically. While there is nothing wrong with using these, should you feel the desire, most people tend to rely upon their experience instead. Apart from being far less complicated, it is generally far more accurate! Thus, once again, it is important that you practise the estimation of time whenever possible. You will find, for example, that whereas small or shallow descents are usually ignored, you will need to add about 4 minutes for every 100 m of height lost where the descent is steep or exceptionally long.

Accurate time estimation is a mixture of mathematics and experience. Naismith's Rule should be seen as a way of giving an approximation of time; experience should then tell you when to add or subtract a few minutes. Some people work out a 'percentage error' on the first few legs of the walk and then use this to further adjust all later calculations that day. Others, realising that high level mountain walking can be fairly strenuous at times, take tiredness into consideration and increase their timings slowly throughout the day. You should adopt a method which best suits you, finding this method through experience, and using Naismith's Rule as a starting point rather than the be-all and end-all of time estimation.

To recap: The ability to estimate the duration of any leg of navigation is another useful poor visibility technique. A reasonably accurate time can be calculated by using Naismith's Rule, this estimate being made more precise by adding or subtracting time according to the conditions and the terrain.

3.7 **Poor visibility navigation**

Few people who have not experienced real 'white-out' conditions can appreciate just how dangerous they can be. A true white-out can occur only in snowy conditions, and is a combination of snow on the ground, heavily falling snow, mist and wind. Under these circumstances it is sometimes literally impossible to tell the difference between the snow on the ground and the snow in the air. This tends to have a number of effects. Firstly, you can become extremely disorientated and will probably fall over a fair amount. Secondly, your companions will appear to next to float. Thirdly, you could be standing on the lip of a precipice without even realising it was there. Conditions as extreme as this are rare south of the Scottish Highlands, except in winter, but mountain mist combined with stormy conditions can be almost as difficult and dangerous, and can occur in any area and at any time of year. With experience and knowledge of the correct procedures, it is possible for you to navigate accurately under all these conditions.

It has been emphasised that, in fine weather, you should be able to navigate using map interpretation alone. In poor conditions, especially those in which the visibility is reduced to next to nothing, you may have to make use of the additional techniques such as bearings, pacing and timing. In addition to these, there are a number of other things which you can do to make life a little easier.

a. *Preparation*
Study the map carefully the evening before you plan to go on the

walk and prepare a route card. This should not be long-winded – you do not have to write a piece of descriptive prose – but it should contain all the necessary facts such as *magnetic* bearings, timings, etc., as outlined earlier in the book.

You should not be afraid to use your escape routes if conditions begin to close in with a vengeance; only fools press on regardless. If the going starts to get rough, turn back well before you reach your limit while you still have enough energy left. Do not forget that if the wind was behind you on your outward journey, it will be against you on your way back, and this will make your position even more difficult. Be safe – know and follow the Mountain Code (see Appendix I), and think about mountain safety (see Appendix III).

You will find it useful to have easy access to everything you need. Your compass is best kept on a neck- or wrist-loop, and your map should either be kept in a waterproof map case designed for use in the mountains, or you can waterproof it yourself by covering it with clear, self-adhesive plastic film or placing it inside a polythene bag, although this is not so effective. It is best to fold the map in such a way that you can see the area in which you are walking without having to open it out fully. Anyone who has tried to read or refold a fully open map even in a light breeze will tell you how difficult it can be.

b. *Concentration*

Good navigation requires concentration. Insist that you are not unnecessarily interrupted by your companions. Keep the party together and appoint someone reliable as a 'back marker'. His job is to look after the group, ensuring that no-one strays, leaving you to concentrate totally on the navigation. He should also make sure that you are not going too fast; in mountain walking you should always travel at the pace of the slowest member of the party. Remember that group leadership and management are particularly important in poor conditions.

Be alert for possible errors in your navigation or route finding, and try to correct them as early and as accurately as you can. It is a good idea to have someone check your bearing as you go along.

Theoretically, this should be the back marker, but in practice this is often impossible because the visibility may be so bad that your back marker cannot see you! He also has the responsibility of keeping tabs on the rest of the group. When this situation occurs, get the third person in the line to check that you are on course; the person immediately behind you will be too close to be accurate. Obviously, whoever checks your bearing should be as experienced as you in using a compass.

The worse the visibility becomes, the more important it is to keep the party together, and the more difficult it will be for you to sight on objects to give you your direction of travel. In extremely bad conditions you may have to resort to a technique known as *leap-frogging*, which is described in detail in section 3.9.

c. Observation

Keep your eyes open for anything which will pinpoint your position or confirm that you are on course. Your ears can be useful as well as your eyes – rivers are usually noisy! Keep each leg of navigation as short as possible, around 500 m as a maximum, for the longer the leg, the greater any error. It is easy to misread a bearing by a couple of degrees, and this error could be compounded by mistakes made while following the bearing. A $6°$ error over a distance of 1 km will throw you off target by about 100 m. If the visibility is down to 20 m (which it could easily be in the mountains), you will have no chance whatsoever of seeing your target. This is where your other skills, such as pacing and timing, play an extremely important role.

Let us assume that you are about to follow a bearing in very poor visibility. You have worked out how many minutes this particular leg of navigation should take, and you have also measured the distance so that you will be able to pace it. You set off confidently along your bearing, but after the estimated amount of time has

Mountain (glacial) lakes often occur below spurs, ridges and the back walls of cwms/corries. By taking a compass bearing on them (or, more accurately, on some definite feature such as their outflow), you can pinpoint your position on the ridge above. Location = SO/000218. View approximately $047°$ Mag.

elapsed, and you have paced out the estimated distance, there is no sign of your target within your range of vision. You might feel you have underestimated on the time, in which case you could carry on for a short while, certainly not more than 100 m, so long as there is nothing potentially dangerous shown on the map in front of you. Either way, eventually you will have to stop and look carefully at what you can see of the surrounding terrain, using your map interpretation skills. If, for example, your objective is situated on the crest of a ridge and you see that, having climbed up, you are now heading downhill again, it should seem fairly obvious that you have overshot. In this case you should retrace your steps *using a back bearing* until you regain the crest of the ridge. If the target is still nowhere to be seen, or if the terrain is such that you get no clues as to the whereabouts, direction or proximity of your objective, you will have to carry out a *sweep search* as described in the next section.

To recap: it is possible for the visibility in the mountains to become almost non-existent. In this situation you could be standing on the edge of a precipice without realising it. It is at times like these when you will need to use a variety of techniques. Preparation will help, but you will also need to concentrate on the task in hand, and be observant.

3.8 **Sweep searches**

Sweep searches, illustrated in Fig. 19, can be an effective way of recovering from slight errors of navigation. For reasons which will become obvious, they are more effective the greater the number of people taking part in them.

The basic idea is that the party should spread out into a line, each person (except the two people at either end) making sure that they can see *both* their neighbours. The best way to ensure this is for each person to go to the limit of his neighbour's visibility, and then come back a few paces. The member of the party who takes up position at one end of the line should be standing at the exact spot

101

Sweep searches

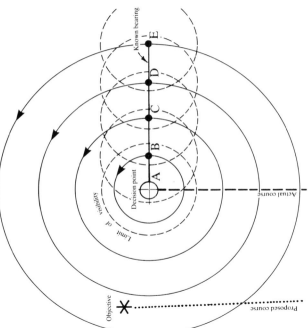

Fig. 19. Initial sweep search.

Stage one. When the decision point has been reached, the group should spread out in a line along a known bearing. No person should go beyond the limit of visibility of his neighbour(s). Person A stays at the decision point, and should always be able to see person B. Person B should always be able to see persons A and C, etc.

Stage two. The line should now rotate around person A until either the objective has been sighted (as shown in this diagram) or until a full sweep of 360° has been made.

Stage three. If the objective is not sighted in the first sweep, further sweeps will be necessary. This procedure is shown in Fig. 20.

reached when the decision to make a sweep search was taken, and he should take a compass bearing along the line of people. The whole line now moves, pivoting around the person who is standing (and stays standing) on the original course, until, if you're lucky, the target is found. If, after a full sweep of 360°, when the line of people will be back on the bearing taken by the 'pivot man', the target still has not been sighted, you will have to think back very carefully to see if you can identify any error in your navigation. If you still feel that you are near to the target, you can carry out further sweeps, but these will get more complex the more you do, for you should always be able to regain the 'decision point'.

Perhaps the most straightforward way to carry out further sweeps is to line the party up as before, take a bearing along the line of people, then pace out the distance between one and the other. The line then pivots around the person at the far end, who must not move. If this second sweep proves unsuccessful, you can regain your original position by following a back bearing along the line for the required number of paces. Using this system, it is possible to do as many sweeps as required to find the target. The important thing to remember is that you should always know the distance and bearing of the 'pivot man' from the 'decision point' (see Fig. 20).

3.9 **Leap-frogging**

When walking on a bearing in conditions of extremely poor visibility, you may be faced with the problem that you can see no obvious features on which to sight your compass. In this situation, you will have to use one of the members of your party as the feature!

Send someone off in front of you until they just reach your limit of visibility, then get them to walk back a couple of paces so that you can sight on them more easily, and so there is no danger of their disappearing from view if the mist thickens. Now sight along the compass in the normal way, and ask the person acting as your feature to move to the right or left until they are standing exactly on course. The whole party can now move to that position, and the

Leap frogging

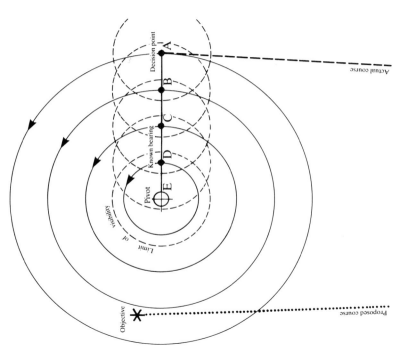

Fig. 20. Further sweep searches. The procedure is exactly the same as in the initial sweep search, except that the sweep is made from a position other than the decision point. You should always be able to regain this decision point. This can be done by measuring the bearing and distance between the first and last person in the line. The sweep is then made around the last person in the line. When the full sweep of 360° has been made, the decision point can be regained by pacing the distance from the pivot man along the calculated bearing.

procedure is then repeated. You must make sure that you take your next bearing from the precise position at which your 'human feature' was standing.

If there are two experienced navigators in the party, one can sight on the other, then walk past him until the limit of his visibility is reached, and so on (hence the name of the technique). This procedure is illustrated in Fig. 21.

Although this technique is extremely time-consuming, easily doubling any estimate of time made from Naismith's Rule, when done correctly it does provide a means of navigating with extreme accuracy in conditions of exceptionally poor visibility.

3.10 Passing obstacles

In straight-line navigation you will sooner or later be faced with some obstacle which prevents you from continuing along your chosen course. If the visibility is good enough, and you can see an obvious feature which lies directly on course on the other side of this obstacle, you can simply walk around until you reach this feature and then carry on as usual. If there is no obvious feature, but you can see a way of passing the obstacle which lies within your range of visibility for its entire length, you should send a member of your party to the other side, sight him on your compass until he is directly on course and then move the rest of the party across to join him.

Inevitably, there will come a time when neither of the above options is available. In this situation you will be forced to make a detour. When this happens it is imperative that the detour is made in such a way that you can regain your original course once you have passed the obstacle. The procedure you should follow is fairly straightforward, if somewhat lengthy, and is illustrated in Fig. 22.

If you have not already done so, you should first make a note of your present bearing. Now have a good look at the 'lie of the land' (or as much of it as you can see), and point the direction of travel arrow along a route which lies parallel to the obstacle. Turn the compass housing until you have set the magnetic bearing on that

Passing obstacles

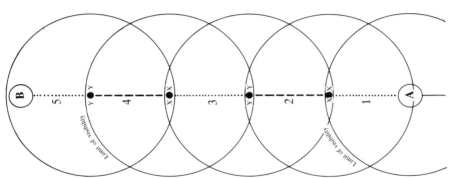

Fig. 21. Leap-frogging. In this example we assume there are two experienced navigators in the group, persons **X** and **Y**.

1. Person **X** walks to just within the limit of visibility. Person **Y** then sights him on the compass and tells him to move to the left or right until he is standing directly on course.

2. The group walks to person **X** who stands still. Person **Y** walks past him to just within the limit of visibility. Person **X** then sights him on the compass and tells him to move to the left or right until he is standing directly on course. The group now move to person **Y** who stands still.

3. Repeat Stage 1.

4. Repeat Stage 2.

5. Continue until the objective is in sight.

105

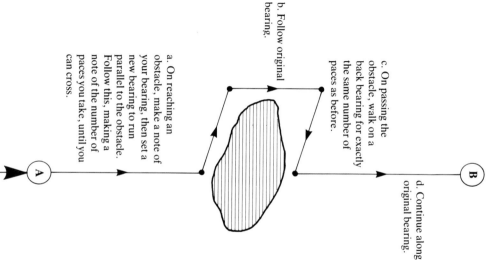

a. On reaching an obstacle, make a note of your bearing, then set a new bearing to run parallel to the obstacle. Follow this, making a note of the number of paces you take, until you can cross.

b. Follow original bearing.

c. On passing the obstacle, walk on a back bearing for exactly the same number of paces as before.

d. Continue along original bearing.

Fig. 22. Passing obstacles.

course (i.e. until the red end of the needle lies directly over the orienting arrow), and follow this new bearing until you find a place where you can get across/around/over, making a note of the number of paces it took you to get there. Now pass the obstacle on your original bearing, remembering to count your paces if you have been step counting previously. Once across, reset your compass to exactly the same bearing as the one you used to walk parallel to the obstruction, then follow a back bearing for precisely the same number of paces as before. If you have been accurate, you will now be back on course again, but on the far side of the obstruction. Make sure that you allow for this detour in any time estimation.

3.11 **Aiming off**

If your objective is a suitable feature, you may find it useful to aim deliberately to one side of it! This is a technique known as 'aiming off', and can be used when the point for which you are making is, or lies on, a linear feature such as a stream, a track or the junction of two field boundaries. If, for example, you are heading for a stream junction, you can deliberately aim either upstream or downstream of the exact point.

The reasoning behind the use of this technique is simple.

Assuming that the stream lies across your path in some way, any slight error in navigation would take you to the stream but not the junction. Once there, you would have no idea whether the junction was upstream or downstream of you. According to that well-known and ever-present rule known as 'Sod's Law', you can almost guarantee that you will choose to walk in the wrong direction, and then have to retrace your steps. By deliberately aiming off, you have a far better chance of choosing the right direction. This technique is illustrated in Fig. 23.

Under normal circumstances it would be better to aim off to the upstream side of the junction so that you are then able to walk downhill to get to your objective. However, you should think about the way in which you use this technique for, if your subsequent route lies down the stream to, for example, a second stream

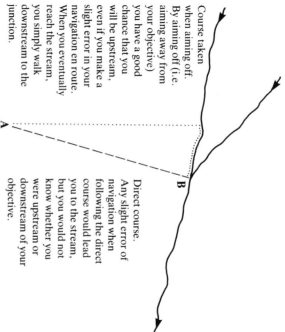

Fig. 23. Aiming off.

Course taken when aiming off. By aiming off (i.e. aiming away from your objective) you have a good chance that you will be upstream, even if you make a slight error in your navigation en route. When you eventually reach the stream, you simply walk downstream to the junction.

Direct course. Any slight error of navigation when following the direct course would lead you to the stream, but you would not know whether you were upstream or downstream of your objective.

junction or a pool, it is pointless gaining height simply to lose it again. Whatever your next objective, take this into consideration when deciding to which side you are going to aim off, and try not to gain or lose any height unnecessarily. Obviously, if you feel you need to pace or time the following leg of navigation, you will have to reach the exact position of the target on this leg, but there are bound to be times when your next route will be well defined.

3.12 Aspect of slope

Let us assume that you are standing at the top of a slope, not knowing your exact position, but wanting to descend. You see from your map that it is 'safe' to descend at one point, but not at any other. If this 'safe' slope faces a slightly different direction to that of the 'unsafe' slopes, you can use your compass to find out where to descend. This is known as measuring the *aspect* of the slope.

Place your compass on the map with the direction of travel arrow pointing down the 'safe' slope and at right angles to the contour lines. Take a grid bearing from this position and convert it to a magnetic bearing. Now walk along the top of the slope pointing the direction of travel arrow directly downhill until the red end of the needle lies directly over the orienting arrow. When this happens you will – in theory – be standing at the top of the 'safe' slope. However, when the difference in aspect of the 'safe' and 'unsafe' slopes is only slight, extremely accurate map interpretation and compass work are needed, and this technique requires much practice to be accurate in what could be a critical situation. When descending the 'safe' slope, *be careful*, and keep your eyes open. You may have made a small error which has led you towards the top of a cliff.

This technique can also be used when, for example, you are contouring around the head of a valley and wish to strike off at a particular point. By measuring the aspect of slope at the point at which you wish to change course, then checking your position as you go along, you will know exactly when to leave your contouring course for your new course. There are innumerable other applications which, at this stage, I feel should be left to your own imagination!

3.13 Attack points

Sometimes it may happen that the particular point for which you are trying to make is not an obvious feature. Even if it is, it may lie in a difficult position, or may even be impossible to reach directly from your present position owing to some obstacle lying across your path. All this, of course, should be fairly obvious from the map. When this happens, one way around the problem is to aim off, as described earlier, but you will find it difficult to do this if the point does not lie on or near a linear feature.

One answer is to approach your objective via an intermediate point, known as an *attack point*, which you can reach with relative ease. From this point, a combination of bearing and pacing will enable you to reach your target far more simply than if you were to head straight for it. In many ways, the use of attack points is an extension of the route-finding skills discussed earlier.

Referring to Fig. 24, let us assume that you are standing at the trig point (A) in conditions of fairly poor visibility, and you wish to get to the pool (B). Obviously, you cannot use the direct route because of the large cliff lying directly across your path. Walking direct and making a detour would be a lengthy and fairly complicated procedure and, although it could be done, not only is it not advisable to walk directly towards the edge of a cliff in poor visibility, but there is a far better alternative available which makes use of an attack point (X).

What you should do is use your map to work out the grid bearing from your present position to the attack point. However, note how the attack point lies at the end of a linear feature (the junction of the field boundaries). If you followed a direct bearing and reached the boundary with the junction nowhere in sight, you would not know whether to walk to the left or right. Therefore, this is another situation where the technique of aiming off will be useful. The visibility is decreasing all the time, so you decide to leap-frog to the attack point. Once you have reached the field boundary, and walked along it to the junction, you can then calculate a further bearing which will take you to the pool. It would be advisable to estimate the distance and step count. (Note how, in this example, we are using a number of different techniques in combination with one another.)

If, during your journey to the attack point, the visibility starts to improve and you catch a glimpse of the pool, there is no reason why you should not head straight for it, so long as *a*, you are sure that it is the right pool, and *b*, you can see that you are well past the dangerous ground where the cliff curves around. If you do decide that it is safe for you to proceed directly, take a compass bearing on the pool and stay heading directly for it. If the visibility starts to

Attack points

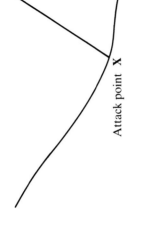

Attack point **X**

B

A

Fig. 24. Attack points. For explanation, see text.

close in again, you can always follow this bearing. If you are forced to detour by the marshy ground, keep your eyes on the weather and, if it looks as though the visibility is going to close in, check that your bearing to the pool is still correct.

Once you have walked away from your original route, you should always have some point of reference which can be used if the visibility suddenly drops. If the worst comes to the worst, and the mist takes you unawares by hiding the pool before you have a chance to take a bearing, you could always work out an approximate course from the area in which you are standing to the field boundary, and proceed from there. However, having to do something like this should be regarded as bad practice, for there will come a time when there is no obvious linear feature which you can use to get you out of trouble.

3.14 **Handrails**

One of the easiest and most effective means of navigating in the mountains (and anywhere else, for that matter) is to use *handrails* whenever possible. These are simply well defined linear features such as paths, tracks, field boundaries, streams, edges of forests, narrow valleys, sharp ridges and even contour lines (but see the comments about following contours in section 3.16). Most of the 'great explorers' used handrail navigation when, for example, they followed rivers into unknown territory. In South America, not only did the Amazon give relatively easy access into the interior, it also provided a very useful and much needed reference point which enabled them to get back to civilisation again (sometimes!).

A bearing can be seen as a type of handrail; after all, it is really only an imaginary straight line. Because following bearings takes a certain amount of concentration, you may find that you prefer to

Even in remote mountain areas, it is often possible to find evidence of past quarrying or mining activities. Remains of inclines and tramways (for example) can provide useful 'handrails' when ascending from the valley floor to the tops. Location = SH/681459. View approximately 053° Mag.

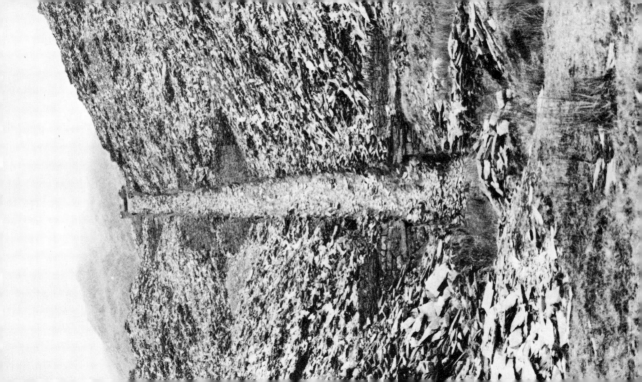

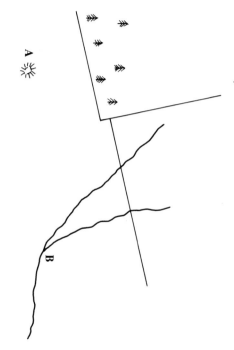

Fig. 25. Handrails. While it would be possible to aim off and follow a compass bearing, it is easier, especially in poor visibility, to follow the handrails formed by the forest, the field boundary and the stream.

use natural handrails whenever they are available. Certainly, in clear conditions, when your compass is stuck firmly in your pocket for much of the day, they can be a great aid to map interpretation and a means of quickly and easily getting from one position to another without having to spend all your time with your nose in a map.

For an example of the way in which you can use handrails to your advantage, have a look at Fig. 25. Let us assume that you are standing by the cairn at point A, and you want to get to the stream junction at point B. There is, of course, nothing to stop you taking a bearing on the junction itself, or, better still, aiming off. If the visibility is particularly poor, you may be forced to leap-frog along the bearing, and this is going to take time and effort. In this particular situation there is an obvious handrail (the edge of the forest) to the north. All you have to do is head in a general northerly direction until you reach the forest, then turn right (eastwards) until you reach the field boundary. Once there, follow the field boundary until you reach the stream, then follow this down to the junction. You have only had to consult your compass once, and then very briefly in order to give you a general direction, right at the start.

3.15 Relocation

A good mountain navigator is never lost; he may be 'temporarily mislocated', but he is *never* lost! Whatever you think about the truth of this statement (and, all things being equal, it should be true), it is very important that you realise how much your mental attitude will affect your decisions when, for some reason which is totally inexplicable at the time, you find yourself 'temporarily mislocated'.

You may be a superb and accurate navigator, but it is almost certain that you will make a mistake at some time during your life. Unless you are prepared for the eventuality, it will come as rather a shock.

Let us assume you have been leap-frogging on a bearing which is supposed to take you to an isolated pool. According to your watch, you are well over the time you estimated it would take you to get there, even allowing for the fact that you have been forced to use a time-consuming technique in order to follow the bearing. Not only that, you have been pacing as well, and you know that you have overshot the estimated distance by about 150 m. The temptation will be to carry on in the hope that the pool lies directly ahead only a few minutes away, but you must have the mental courage to stop, sit down and try to work things out.

The first thing to do is tell yourself that you are *not* lost! The last thing you need now is a brain made useless by panic. Think about your route; try to remember any features passed along the way that might help you relocate yourself. Look at the ground within your range of visibility to see if that gives you any clues. If, for example, your target is a stream junction, it will be located in a valley of some description. If, on the other hand, it is a trig point, it will be on fairly high ground.

If you are still as puzzled as you were before, now is the time to go through all your calculations again with a fine tooth comb. Check your estimates of time and distance, and make sure the bearing on your compass agrees with the one on your route card. If everything seems correct, check the bearing again by recalculating it from the map. You may have made an error the night before when writing your route card: a common mistake is forgetting to allow for the magnetic variation. If you can still find nothing wrong, you will have to do one or more sweep searches. Remember to conduct these searches in such a way that you can always get back to your decision point; in a situation such as this it is your only point of reference. If your bearing was incorrect, work out the position to which that bearing would have taken you, and study the map to see if there are any definite features in that area which would help you relocate yourself.

Assuming that all your calculations were correct and that you followed the bearing accurately, you should find the target during one of the sweeps. If not, keep calm. Ask yourself various questions. Did you start this leg of navigation from the correct position? If you started from a particular feature, are there any similar features nearby which might have confused you? In misty conditions, one stream junction looks very much like another. If it is possible that you started from the wrong position, where would your course put you now? Are there are any identifiable features in this position which would help you relocate yourself? If not, what would happen if you continued along your present course? Are there any identifiable features on this course which would help you relocate yourself?

Does your map mention any magnetic anomalies in the area? Does your compass needle point to the same place as everyone else's? (When checking this, keep fairly well spread out because one compass will affect another.) Is it possible that your compass has been affected by anything metallic or magnetic? Are you wearing a metallic watch strap? If it appears that you have been following the wrong bearing because your compass has proved faulty in some way, try to work out the bearing on which you have been walking. (Be careful when doing this because the error may not have been constant.) Where does this new bearing place you? Are there any recognisable features in this area that would help you to relocate yourself?

Is it possible that your map might be wrong? Is it possible that the feature for which you are searching no longer exists? Streams can change course, field boundaries can be demolished, trig points can be moved, mountain pools can dry up. If this may have happened, are there any other identifiable features in the area which will help you relocate yourself?

You will by now have noted, whatever the line of inquiry, that you always end up asking about the possibility of identifiable features. This is no coincidence, for the only way to locate yourself accurately in this situation is to find such a feature.

After all these questions, if you still feel there is no hope of finding your target or relocating yourself, you will be forced to escape from the situation in some way. Assuming that you have kept your legs of navigation reasonably short, you should be able to work out your approximate position (to within, say, 1500 m). What you now need to find is some long and obviously well defined linear feature which is certain to cross your path if you head towards it. This can be a road, the edge of a forest, a long field boundary, a river or valley, or even the *base* of a cliff. Obviously, you should not head towards the top of a cliff. In fact, you should head in a direction which, if possible, avoids any potentially dangerous areas.

Referring to your 1:25,000 scale map of Abergavenny and the Black Mountains, let us assume that you are temporarily mislocated on Mynydd Llangattock, somewhere in the region of grid square 1814. You had been heading for the cairn at 187147. In your sweep searches, not only have you not found the cairn, you have also not found any sign of the stony ground shown to the west of it. Having decided that there is no hope of finding the target, you look for an obvious escape feature which does not involve heading towards any potentially dangerous ground. You would clearly not head north

because of the cliffs, and there is a large area of old workings and generally rough ground to the south. The obvious feature is the road to the west and reaching it involves you in no potential dangers. No matter where you are on Llangattock Mountain, if you head in a westerly direction you will eventually reach the road.

Should you be unfortunate enough to find yourself in this type of situation in worsening weather conditions, and in an area which is ringed with potential dangers, you may well have to face the fact that the most advisable course of action is to find some shelter and 'sit it out'. The ultimate responsibility is yours, and you will have to choose your course of action according to the factors affecting you at the time. Whatever you decide to do, try to keep calm and work through the problems systematically and rationally.

Ideally, if you concentrate on what you are doing and double check each move before you make it, you will never find yourself in the unenviable position of having to make such a decision.

3.16 **Some other considerations**

a. *Pace*

Try to keep to a steady pace. This can be difficult in poor conditions, but it does help you to estimate time more accurately. Additionally, if you are leading a group and you keep to a steady pace instead of constantly faltering, the rest of the party will feel confident in your ability which, in turn, will help you.

b. *Following contours*

Although, in general, it is not a good idea to follow contours (i.e. to traverse), it is often useful and sometimes necessary. When traversing steep ground you will automatically tend to lose height and you should, therefore, try to make allowances for it. However,

Not only is there an obvious cairn (right centre) which will help you locate yourself, there is also a line of electricity pylons which can be used as a linear feature with which to set the map. Remember not to use magnetic bearings when standing below either a pylon or the cables. Location = SO/147159. View approximately 170° Mag.

most people who realise this fact tend to over-compensate and gain height! Only practice and experience can show you where the balance lies.

c. *Descending mist*

For most of the time, assuming fair visibility, you should be navigating using the map alone. If you are doing this and you notice that mist or cloud is closing in rapidly, you should immediately do four things:

1. Get your party together.
2. Try to work out your exact position.
3. Take a bearing on some obvious feature which you can identify on the map and which lies on or near your objective, *or – better still –* take a bearing on your objective, if you can see it, *or,* if you can still see your starting point, work out the bearing from this point to your target and, by using a back bearing, get on course.
4. Follow this bearing.

d. *Map and compass*

Always work on the assumption that your map and compass are correct, bearing in mind the limitations which have already been mentioned (i.e. the age of the map and magnetic anomalies). If a feature is not in the position at which you expected to find it, the most likely explanation is that you have made a mistake. Human errors and the incorrect use of compasses are far more common than map errors and magnetic anomalies.

e. *Night navigation*

Navigating at night is like navigating in conditions of poor visibility. Use handrails whenever possible, and think carefully about aiming off and attack points before following a bearing. A head torch will prove invaluable, but try to keep its use to a minimum. It takes a long time for your eyes to adapt to night vision, but they will change back to normal vision almost instantaneously if the light level increases above a certain point. When following bearings, you may well have to resort to leap-frogging. If it is a very dark night, the person on whom you sight may well have to show some kind of light. If, however, it is a clear night, you can use a star, low on the horizon, as a sighting point (make sure you can recognise it again). Because stars are not stationary with respect to the horizon, you should change your point of reference at least once every 15 minutes.

f. *Stellar navigation*

If you are not heading along a precise bearing but wish to check your approximate direction, you can find north on a clear night without the use of a compass by looking for the Pole Star. Its position is indicated by the 'pointers' of The Plough, a constellation which most people can recognise. Do not make the mistake of thinking that the Pole Star is very bright – it isn't! Fig. 26 should help you to work out the correct position.

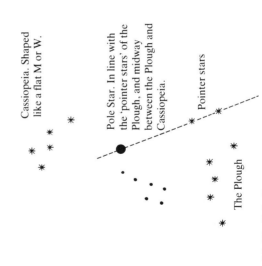

Cassiopeia. Shaped like a flat M or W.

Pole Star. In line with the 'pointer stars' of the Plough, and midway between the Plough and Cassiopeia.

Pointer stars

The Plough

Fig. 26. The Pole Star.

g. *Solar navigation*

If you are not heading along a precise bearing during the day but wish to check your approximate direction, you can find south without the aid of a compass by using your wrist watch – as long as it is not digital, and shows the correct time! The procedure is straightforward. Ignore the minute hand, and point the hour hand directly at the sun. South is mid-way between the hour hand and 12 o'clock. This technique is only accurate in Britain using Greenwich Mean Time, so you should remember to take away 1 hour from the time in summer because of British Summer Time.

h. *Improvised techniques*

The sun is always slightly to the south in the British Isles. In thaw conditions, snow will therefore usually melt faster on south-facing slopes. Mosses and other plants which like shade will tend to grow more profusely on the north-facing sides of walls. Because the prevailing winds in Britain are from the south-west most exposed trees and shrubs will be bent towards the north-east. There are any number of 'laws of the countryside' which can be used as improvised direction finders.

3.17 **A word of caution**

Once you have read, digested and understood all the principles and techniques described in Parts Two and Three, you will be in a position where you can *start* to learn about mountain navigation. It does not matter whether you go into the mountains in summer or winter: the basic principles remain the same throughout the year. However, in general terms, navigation is usually far more involved during winter and early spring, because not only are you more likely to experience inclement weather, but also many of

Navigating in winter conditions can be somewhat more difficult than during the summer months. Many obvious features can disappear under a covering of snow. This group is following what, in summer, is a well defined path!
Location = SH/652595. View approximately 130° Mag.

the features which you would use during the summer months may well be hidden under a covering of snow.

Obviously, there is a host of other things which you will need to know and to have experienced before you can think of yourself as a capable mountain-goer. You will, for example, need to have a good understanding of mountain weather, of safety considerations and techniques, and of the use of ropes (not necessarily confined to rock-climbing situations). If you intend to venture into the mountains in winter, a basic knowledge of snow- and ice-climbing techniques will prove invaluable, and it is essential that you know how to use an ice axe and crampons correctly and efficiently. You should also know about winter survival and the causes of avalanches. Unfortunately, such considerations are outside the scope of this book.

As was said right at the beginning, reading the book and gaining the knowledge are, by themselves, not enough. *You must gain practical experience.* So far as the navigation techniques are concerned, no matter where you live you should be able to find somewhere to practise them, even if, at the outset, you have to visit the local park. Eventually, you should aim to gain experience of the full range of skills encompassed by the term 'mountaincraft' while in a mountain area. During your first few trips, you would be well advised to do this with an experienced leader, whether through a group of friends, a mountaineering club or one of the growing number of mountain activities centres which can be found in every mountain area in Britain. You will find a number of useful addresses in Appendix V.

Part four
Orienteering

4.1 What is orienteering?

One of the recurrent themes of this book so far has been the importance of practical experience. While you must obviously get most of this experience in a mountain environment, preferably with someone more experienced than yourself, one of the most effective and enjoyable ways in which you can practise your map interpretation skills is by taking part in the increasingly popular sport of orienteering.

In certain parts of the world, particularly in some of the Scandinavian countries, orienteering is followed with the same sort of fervour as is rugby in Wales. In Britain it appears to be regarded, along with rock climbing, caving, hang-gliding, etc., as a 'minor sport'. This is a great pity, for it has a lot to recommend it. One of the most attractive features of the sport is that any person of any age can participate at whatever level they wish. At international standard, it can be highly competitive and gruelling; at the general 'weekend amateur' level, it has similarities with mountain-walking.

An orienteering event can be likened to a social stroll led by a guide who does not come with you, but gives you a map of features of interest and then asks you to confirm that you have been to them. He leaves the choice of route between the features entirely up to you, and leaves a control flag with a special card punch in an obvious position at each feature. The sport is therefore a combination of map reading and walking. The competitive element is to see who can complete the walk and find all the features in the fastest time, and you are therefore asked to go alone. To compete with any degree of success at regional or international events, you will need to be fairly skilled at map interpretation and various navigation techniques, and you will also have to do some running between the various features, or 'controls'.

If you do not feel like running, and wish only to have a

pleasurable stroll in the country, there are the 'wayfaring courses', some permanent, many being held at the same time as other levels of competition, and in the same area. These have no competitive element apart from that of pitting your wits against the course designer. Both in this and in the more competitive events, the more advanced the course, the more cunning is the placement of the various controls.

A further attraction of the sport is that most events take place well off the beaten track, often in areas which would otherwise be inaccessible to the casual walker or visitor. Special permission is often granted to orienteering clubs so that they can stage events in normally private land; indeed, one of the prime requirements for a good orienteering 'course' is that the participants should not know the area beforehand.

While it is beyond the scope of this book to give full details, a few words on the subject may serve to persuade even the most staid mountain-walking die-hards to give the sport a try! Further details are available from the British Orienteering Federation, whose address can be found in Appendix V, or from some of the books listed in Appendix VI.

4.2 Clothing and equipment

You will not need anything special for orienteering (unless you get really competitive) apart from a protractor-compass, and this you should already have for your mountain-walking. In fact, you could wear your mountain-walking clothing, but many people prefer a track-suit and trainers with, perhaps, a lightweight cagoule for inclement conditions. You should note that British Orienteering Federation rules state that arms and legs must be covered, so shorts and running-vests should not be worn.

In addition to the clothing, you should take with you a couple of biros of different colours (or chinagraph pencils if it's wet), a large plastic bag in which to put your map, your protractor-compass and (BOF rules, again) a whistle. It's a good idea to take a change of clothing and a towel, and some food and a flask of warm drink. The courses often cross rough ground, and if the weather is unkind you will almost certainly get wet and muddy. Most events are held well off the beaten track, and there will often be no changing facilities apart from the back of your car.

The entry fee for each event varies, but it covers the cost of the map, a control card and control description card (see later), and the organisers will also send you the results of the competition, unless you followed only the wayfaring course.

4.3 The events

A typical orienteering event is a combination of a number of different courses, each designed specifically for a particular level of competition. Because it is obviously important that you should not be able to 'cheat' by following other competitors, most events are held in wooded areas or scrubby heathlands.

If you are going along for the first time and would like to have a go, you will be welcomed at any event other than an international or championship meeting, or a 'closed' event. If, after your first few tries, you find you like the sport and wish to take part in competitions, you will have to join one of the many orienteering clubs. The annual subscription will give you affiliation to the regional association and the British Orienteering Federation, which means you will be eligible to compete in any event on the BOF fixture list. You also get a bi-monthly magazine (*The Orienteer*), insurance and all the things you would expect from a large, national sporting body.

The competitions are divided, by age groups, into eleven different categories. If there is an exceptionally large number of people entering for one particular category, there may be two or more courses labelled A, B, C, etc. Many clubs are now using colour-coded courses as these are not dependent on age. The code relates more to the difficulty than to the length of each course, the six categories running from white (easy, up to 3 km) through yellow, orange, green and red to blue (hard and long, 7–12 km). There is often, as was mentioned earlier, a wayfaring course as well.

In order to avoid confusion, this will usually have a different start and finish point to the main competitions.

There are, apart from the competition categories, several different types of event. The one which most people think of when they hear about orienteering is the 'cross-country'. In this, the course covers wooded or mixed ground where the markers are given in a specific order. You go from Control 1 to Control 2 and so on. There are then the 'score' events. In these, the controls are not given numbers, but values, the highest value controls being the furthest away (or most difficult to reach) from the start. The idea is that competitors have to get the highest number of points they can within a given time. Points are knocked off for arriving back after that time has elapsed.

A further event is the relay, often staged as a competition between clubs. Each member of each club becomes part of a team, and his time goes towards the average time of his club. This event is probably the most competitive, and is often 'closed'.

Another adaptation of an orienteering event is to hold it at night. Where night meets do take place, they usually cover slightly easier terrain than the equivalent day events. Night orienteering events are only recommended for the experienced!

4.4 The course

When you arrive at the venue, you should go straight to the registration point. When you register, you will have to do so for a particular course. Course distances are stated according to straight line navigation, so if you choose a course of 4 km, by the time you have detoured around obstacles and followed what you consider to be the best route between the controls, you may well find yourself walking 8 km. As soon as you have registered you will receive a starting time, a map, a control card and a control description card. Check that no corrections are needed on the map, and copy any that are.

Once you have sorted yourself out and are ready to go, make your way to the start of the course which may, incidentally, be some distance from the registration area. The route is normally well signposted (sometimes taped). Aim to arrive at the start area about 10 minutes before you are due to set off. Your name will eventually be called, and you will join a queue of competitors who are being sent off at intervals of about 1 minute. By now you should have checked your map to find out its scale and the vertical interval of the contours, and to see if there are any conventional signs which you do not understand. Orienteering maps are slightly different from the standard Ordnance Survey maps, and they have a number of additional conventional signs. They will be described in more detail in the next section.

When you set off, the stub of your control card will be taken as a safety check, and you will find yourself travelling along a well marked course to the master map area. It is here that you will find the maps which tell you the positions of the controls for each course. You should go to the relevant master map and copy the details on to your own. Be as accurate as you can. Each control will have its associated feature marked with a circle, and your control description card will describe not only that feature, but also the exact location of the flag at that feature. For example, the master map may show you a small pool at the circle representing Control 1. The control description card will then tell you that the flag is located on the south side of the pool, or the left bank of the outflow, etc. The circle on the master map gives you the position of that feature and your job is to go and find it. When you reach it, you punch your control card in the correct place, then set off to find the next flag, and so on. Each control will have its own code letters, shown on the flag itself, possibly on the punch, and on your control description card. Always check to make sure you are standing at the correct control.

After you have found all the controls, or made a mistake and run out of time, you make your way to the finish and hand in your control card. It is extremely important that you hand in this card, even if you failed to find any of the controls. At the end of the event, the control cards are tallied with their stubs to make sure that everyone has managed to get back safely. Failure to hand in your control card could result in a search party being called out needlessly.

The whole art of good orienteering is to find the quickest route from one control to another. For the same reasons as were discussed in section 2.7, the quickest route is seldom the shortest. In fact, in orienteering it is probable that the course designer has gone out of his way to make the shortest route one of the slowest.

Finding the quickest route (and one that is relatively easy to follow) takes as much skill as, if not more than, locating the controls themselves, and it is here that you will start to need your map interpretation skills. Successful competitors make much use of such things as linear features, handrails and attack points, and appreciate when the use of bearings, aiming off and pacing can prove advantageous. Map interpretation, however, is still a prerequisite. Without it, you are not going to get very far at all.

4.5 Orienteering maps

There are very few differences between the type of map you use for mountain navigation and the one used for orienteering. If you can read one, you can undoubtedly read the other. However, what differences there are are very important for map interpretation, especially if you want to become successful in competitions.

Because most orienteering maps are drawn specifically for one event, they are usually totally up to date. You will be told about any changes which may have occurred between the time the map was produced and the date of the event when you arrive at the assembly area, and you should obviously mark all these changes on your copy of the map before you start. One of the advantages of having a map which is kept up to date is that it is drawn to magnetic north instead of grid north. This is very important when you come to take bearings from the map. Because the grid lines point towards magnetic north, there is no need to take any magnetic variation into consideration.

Orienteering courses usually take place in fairly difficult terrain, and in order that you be given as many clues as possible, the maps are invariably of a large scale. Scales of from 1:5,000 to 1:20,000 are common. The vertical interval of the contour lines is usually 5 m, but it can vary and you should always check. You may find it useful to make a set of Romer scales for each of the different maps you can expect, or you can purchase a special orienteering compass (Silva type 2NL or 4S) which comes with a set of interchangeable scales which slide on to the front edge of the base plate.

Two of the more immediately noticeable differences on orienteering maps are the use of colour and conventional signs, and the lack of place names. A competitor does not need to know that the stream across his path is known as Muddy Brook, but it would be helpful for him to know the type of vegetation in a particular area. Colours are therefore used to denote vegetation types, visibility and 'runnability'. By looking at these colour codes, an experienced competitor can tell the type of vegetation he must cross, how far he should be able to see in any given direction and how fast he will be able to travel. Because most events take place in forests, where definite features and detailed topographical information are necessary aids to navigation, forests are usually left uncoloured except when it is felt necessary to tell you that they allow good running, or are so dense that it is almost impossible for you to fight your way through them.

Additional conventional signs enable the competitor or 'wayfarer' to identify and locate features which are either too small or too detailed to be shown accurately on the smaller scale Ordnance Survey maps. There are, for example, conventional signs for large boulders, small depressions, ditches, uncrossable walls and crossable fences, many indicating the relative size of the feature (e.g. small stream, large stream). Most of these conventional signs are similar to those used by the Ordnance Survey, and the unique ones are generally self-explanatory. In any case, most orienteering maps carry a key in which all but the most rare signs are explained.

4.6 Following the course

To begin with, the best idea is to take your time, working everything out stage by stage. You may even find that you get round the course far more quickly by walking than by running! Many's the

time that a novice has rushed off into the trees and got lost, only to find that someone who has strolled around the course, thinking about the problems and checking their navigation, has clocked up a faster time. The whole point of the sport is that you must use map interpretation skills to work out your route. While it is impossible for a book to teach you how to become an expert at orienteering, if you think about the poor visibility techniques which were described in Part Three, you will begin to see how they can be used in an orienteering event.

Ask yourself a number of questions before setting off for a control. Remember that you want to find each control both quickly and with the minimum of difficulty. Are there any obvious handrails or combinations of handrails which can be used to reach the control or get nearer to it? If there are a number of choices, does one route offer any significant advantages or disadvantages over the others? Is there an obvious attack point? Do any of the handrails lead you to this attack point? If the control is situated on or near a linear feature, might it be advantageous to aim off? What type of ground lies between you and the control? If one route takes you through thick vegetation (where it will be difficult to travel swiftly), is there a better route? If one route forces you to lose or gain height unnecessarily, is there a more level route? If this route is longer, will it be quicker? Are there any junctions between different types of vegetation which could be used as handrails? Is the competitor who left the map area a short time ago going in the right direction? Is he even following the same course? The more you think about it, the more questions there are to be asked.

To take a practical example, Fig. 27 shows part of a typical orienteering course. You have gone from the start to the master map area, and are just about to set off for Control 1. You see from the master map and the control description card that it is situated at the corner of a fence. Looking at your map, you see that the direct route would force you to cross a deep valley, but that there is a good

In spring, snow often remains on the north-facing side of depressions when the rest of the mountainside is relatively bare. This can be useful as a guide to general direction. Location = SO/140154. View approximately 181° Mag.

track to the south. However, this track only leads you into further difficulties, for there are no definite features which you can use to tell you when to strike off the track towards the control. However, if you go north-west from the master map area you will eventually reach a path. This can be followed north-east to the stream, which in turn can be followed to the fence. If you then follow this fence southwards you will eventually reach the control.

Once you have checked the control code letters to make sure you are standing at the right place, you can punch your control card and start thinking about how to get to the next flag. Your control description card tells you that Control 2 is situated on the southern side of a small pool, and the details you have copied from the master map tell you the location of the pool. Here, again, you have a choice of routes, and it should be fairly obvious that the pool will be difficult to find direct from your present position unless you follow a compass bearing, which is time-consuming. There is, however, an obvious attack point (the stream junction) to the east, and by linking together various linear features it should be reasonably simple to get to the attack point. From there you will have to carefully follow a compass bearing and count paces.

And so it goes on. You arrive at a control, check that it is the correct one, punch your card, and work out what you consider to be the most suitable route to the next control. If you are interested in the competitive side of the sport, you will soon find that you do most of your route evaluation while on the move.

Even if you only go to orienteering events to take part in the wayfaring course, or simply visit one of the growing number of permanent wayfaring courses throughout the country (many of which are listed in Appendix VII), you will find the experience both enjoyable and extremely helpful. Not only will you have a chance to practise your map interpretation skills, you will also have plenty of opportunities to experiment with combinations of other techniques, and it will help you understand why you need to be observant and concentrate on what you are doing.

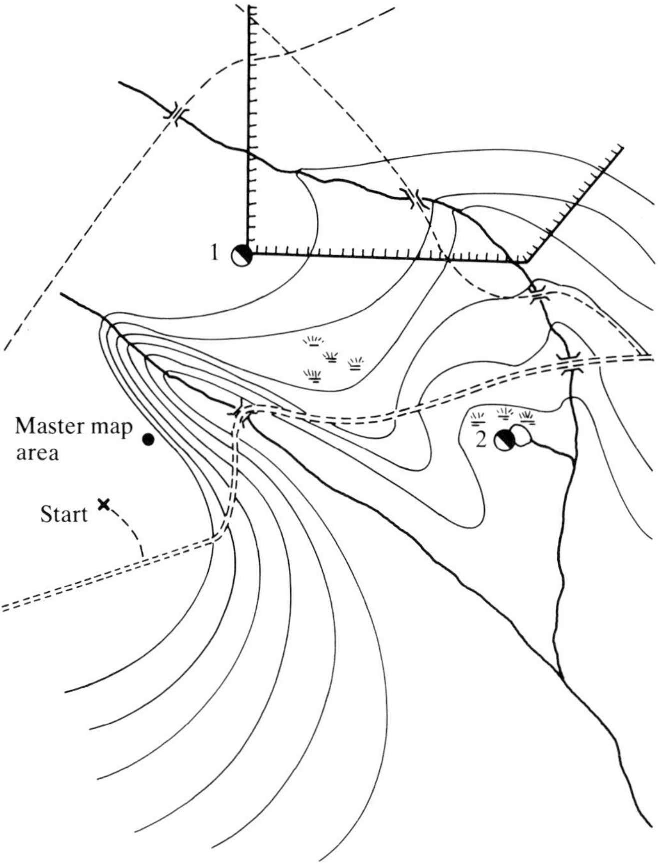

Following the course

Fig. 27. The orienteering course. For explanation, see text.

Appendices

Appendix I The mountain code

Be prepared

Make sure you are correctly clothed and equipped for the proposed walk and the possible weather conditions. Seek advice if you are unsure of what constitutes 'correctly'. Equipment is obviously of little use unless it is sound, and you know how to use it correctly. You should have a reasonable knowledge of basic first aid, and a good knowledge and experience of mountain navigation techniques.

Always carry waterproofs, spare sweater, map and compass, whistle, first aid kit, emergency food (i.e. chocolate, glucose sweets, nuts and raisins – anything with a high calorific value) and a polythene survival bag. In winter you should take extra spare clothing and emergency food, and a good torch. You might also like to split between the group a quality sleeping bag, a stove and a pan in which you can make hot drinks.

Never undertake a walk or expedition which is beyond your training, experience or fitness. Keep to well-known routes until you are proficient at navigation and route finding. You should always check on the rescue facilities available in the area in which you intend to walk. You should know the procedure to use in case of accidents.

It is inadvisable to go into the mountains alone unless you are very experienced. Whether you go alone, with a companion or with a group, it is a good idea to leave details of your route (i.e. a route card) with someone responsible. If you do this, it is extremely important that you report your safe return, for otherwise a rescue team may be called out needlessly.

Check the *local* weather forecast before you set off on your walk, and do not be afraid to alter your plans if the conditions are, or are likely to become, inclement.

Disused mines and quarries in mountainous areas rarely have any safety checks. It is in your own interests to stay well clear of such sites.

Never venture on to snow and ice until you are thoroughly familiar with basic winter techniques. Mastering the use of an ice axe and crampons should be regarded as a *minimum* level of ability. You should understand the cause and effect of such features as cornices and avalanches, especially when walking in the Scottish Highlands where conditions can be severe. Do not forget that winter conditions in Scotland can last from November to May.

In the event of an accident, carry out immediate first aid and get the casualty off the hill. If you cannot do this yourselves, erect a shelter for the casualty and the rest of the group and use the International Mountain Distress Signal (see below). Other people may be nearby and in a position to help. If evacuation is impossible, find a telephone, dial 999 and ask for the police, then ask for Mountain Rescue.

The *International Mountain Distress Signal* is six rapid signals (by whistle, torch, shouting, etc.) repeated at intervals of 1 minute. This should be repeated until you are located. The answer is three rapid signals repeated at intervals of 1 minute.

Respect the land

The designation 'National Park' does not confer any special rights of public ownership or public access on the land. Even in the National Parks, areas of private land exist. Keep to public rights of way and permitted footpaths, especially when travelling in enclosed areas and across land where special access agreements have been made.

All Ordnance Survey maps in common use for mountain navigation have special conventional signs to represent public rights of way, and carry the statement: 'The representation on this map of any other road, track or path is no evidence of the existence of a right of way.' If in doubt about access, seek local advice.

Avoid crossing firing ranges and game-shooting areas. When north of the border, remember the Scottish deer-stalking season (August/September).

If you do not wish to camp on an official camp site, make sure you have the permission of the landowner *before* you pitch your tent. If you dig a hole to make a latrine, replace the turf before moving on.

Appendices

Take care with fires and stoves. There should be nothing to indicate you have camped when you leave.

Take *all* your litter home. If you bury it, animals may dig it up. Empty tins and plastic bags are particularly dangerous to wildlife. Glass bottles are totally unnecessary in the first place.

Conserve wildlife

Do your utmost to disturb neither domestic nor wild animals, and leave flowers and plants for everyone to enjoy. In any case, it is now illegal to pick many wild flowers.

There are agreed closed seasons for various nature reserves and cliff areas, and you should take heed of the notices posted at such places regarding access.

Do not pollute mountain streams by dam-building, dish-washing or any other activity. Any form of pollution can seriously affect the ecology of such streams and their surroundings.

Take *nothing* but photographs.
Leave *nothing* but footprints.
Disturb *nothing* but the air around you.

Consider other people

Never throw stones or any other objects over the tops of crags or down slopes, even if you cannot see anyone below you. There may well be climbers or other walkers hidden from view. If you accidentally dislodge a stone, immediately warn anyone who may be below you, *shouting* the standard call 'Below!'. Even small pebbles falling down a mountainside can gather momentum quickly. These, in turn, can move other stones which may eventually move large boulders.

Many mountaineers leave tents and rucksacks while they go off on a rock climb. Do not remove apparently deserted equipment.

Many people live and work in the mountains. Have consideration for their way of life and their privacy. Mountain streams are often used as the sole water supply for local residents.

Only lead walks and expeditions when you are competent to do so.

Most people go into the mountains to enjoy the peace and quiet of their surroundings. Do nothing that would impinge upon this enjoyment.

Be weatherwise

Even in summer, weather conditions can change with incredible speed. Do not hesitate to turn back if the weather deteriorates; only fools press on regardless. High winds and icing can be serious hazards.

Low cloud or mist will substantially reduce the speed of most parties. Be careful in such conditions. Walk at a speed which allows you to see as much as possible of the ground ahead.

After heavy rain, the crossing of many mountain streams (even by stepping stones or low bridges) may be impossible. Rather than attempting unorthodox crossing methods, you should travel up or down the stream to a safe crossing point.

Both summer and winter weather extremes pose particular problems for mountain walkers. You should know the symptoms and treatment of both heat exhaustion and mountain hypothermia (exhaustion/exposure). You should also know how to avoid such problems.

Walking expeditions in high, craggy mountain areas may require specialist skills, including the use of ropes. Winter mountain-walking, especially in Scotland, can be a most serious undertaking. Apart from the hazards posed by slopes prone to cornices and avalanches, daylight hours are far fewer and general conditions are usually far more extreme than elsewhere in Britain.

(Based upon *The Mountain Code* published by the British Mountaineering Council.)

Appendix II **The country code**

Guard against all risks of fire

Always remove turves before making a fire and ensure that sparks, etc. cannot accidentally set light to surrounding vegetation. Heaths, plantations, woodlands and fellsides are all highly inflammable. The site should be returfed on departure, once you are quite sure that the fire is completely extinguished.

If you discover a fire, efforts should be made to stamp it out. If it is too big for the group to deal with, report the blaze immediately to the fire brigade, police, or Forestry Commission officers.

Leave all gates as you find them
If you are following a public right of way, all gates should be unlocked. If not, there will most likely be a stile nearby. Where there is no stile and the gates are unlocked, open and close them as opposed to climbing over them.

If you open a gate, make sure it is securely closed behind you. Livestock will be drawn to an open gate, and this could have serious consequences.

Keep dogs under proper control
In general terms, you should keep your dog on a lead whenever there is livestock around, and when you are walking along narrow country roads.

Keep to paths across farmland
In areas of enclosed farmland and agreed access areas, follow footpaths carefully. When travelling from valley areas to the open mountain, do everything you can to ensure you find the correct paths.

Recognised routes are usually signposted in some way, either by the standard 'Public Footpath' or 'Public Bridleway' signs, by patches of coloured paint, by a figure of a walking man or by cairns. Long Distance Footpaths are usually waymarked by an 'acorn'. Always use the gates and stiles provided on such routes, even if the path detours to reach them.

On narrow paths, keep in single file.

Avoid damaging fences, hedges and walls
There should be no excuse for crossing a wall, fence or hedge by any other means than a stile or gate if you are on a public footpath.

When on the open mountain, cross dry stone walls via the nearest gate or stile, or detour until you reach a point where you can cross with ease and without risk of causing damage.

Leave no litter

There is no need to carry glass bottles into the country. They are heavy and dangerous.

Take *all* your litter home with you. There is no excuse for leaving anything behind. Leave the countryside as you would wish to find it.

Do not bury litter; animals may dig it up again.

Opened tins, plastic bags and broken glass can be fatal to both domestic and wild animals.

Safeguard water supplies

Many farms and isolated rural communities rely directly on springs as their sole source of drinking water. Do not build dams or pollute the water in any way.

Do not pollute cattle troughs or any other form of water storage or water supply.

Protect wildlife, wild plants and trees

The countryside is best seen, not collected.

Do not pick wild flowers, disturb wild animals or birds, carve your initials on trees or leave graffiti of any description.

Many plants and animals are now protected by law. It is a criminal offence to pick certain wild flowers and to disturb many species of animals and birds.

Go carefully on country roads

Country roads are usually narrow and winding, often with high banks or hedges on either side. When travelling by vehicle, drive slowly and carefully, and be considerate to other road users.

Slow to a crawl if you meet people on horseback. If the road is narrow, stop, and let the horses pass you. Do not rev the engine nor sound the horn.

When walking along country roads, keep to the right and listen for oncoming traffic. Often you will hear a vehicle long before the driver can see you.

Respect the life of the countryside
Many people live and work in the country. Respect the property, livelihood and privacy of local residents.

Always obtain the permission of the landowner before pitching a tent.

Appendix III **Mountain safety**

Every year, people are killed and injured in our mountain areas. Most of these accidents occur because of ignorance, inexperience or sheer stupidity, and are, therefore, avoidable. Perhaps the prime cause of all accidents is a lack of appreciation of the risks inherent in walking or climbing in the mountains, together with a consequent unwillingness to take the trouble to find out how to recognise and deal with potential dangers as and when they do occur. Mountains are not dangerous places in themselves; it is the people who go there who make them dangerous!

Mountain safety is really concerned with simple common sense. Not many people would try deep sea diving without an aqualung, nor would they do anything potentially dangerous in the sea unless they could swim. Similarly, it makes sense that you should not go walking or climbing in the mountains unless you are reasonably fit, properly equipped and aware of all the potential hazards.

In the rest of this appendix we shall look at some of the factors which will affect not only your safety, but also your general comfort, while you are 'on the hill'. Detailed descriptions of the various items of clothing and equipment are outside the scope of this book, but you will find more information in some of the books listed in Appendix VI, or you can get advice from most reputable mountaineering equipment shops.

a. *Footwear*
Boots are essential. Walking shoes, gym shoes, trainers, basketball boots, wellingtons, etc. are not suitable for serious mountain-

walking for a number of reasons. Not only do they provide no ankle support, they also give no protection to the foot when you are walking over rough ground. As with all other equipment, it is best to buy boots which have been designed specifically for use in the mountains. Never buy boots by mail order; have them fitted in the shop (remember to wear the same type of socks as you will when walking), and make sure they are comfortable. There is nothing worse than a pair of ill-fitting boots.

Socks are a matter of personal choice, but most people find they get on best with one pair of thick nylon loopstitch socks, or two pairs of woollen socks. Whatever your personal choice, make sure that the socks fit you well. It is false economy to darn socks for they are invariably uncomfortable and almost always cause blisters.

Even with well-fitting, comfortable boots and shoes, you may suffer from blisters. If you do, try to cover the blister while it is still a 'hot spot' (i.e. before it fills with liquid). If the blister does form, prick it with a sterilised needle (carry a needle in your first aid kit and sterilise it with a match or cigarette lighter), allow the fluid to escape, then cover it well with a padded plaster. If camping in the mountains, allow the blister to get plenty of fresh air whenever possible, as this will help it to harden. Keep your socks clean.

b. *Clothing*

Clothing should be functional and comfortable, and should not restrict movement. Air is an excellent insulator, so the basic idea is to trap as much air as possible. Several layers of thin clothing are therefore far more effective than a couple of layers of thick clothing. This also has the added advantage that it is far easier to keep to a comfortable temperature.

Woollen *underwear* is undoubtedly the best, but many people cannot stand wool next to the skin. In this case, thermal underwear is almost as good. In extreme conditions of cold you will find a pair of 'long-johns' useful, although nylon tights are almost as good! Follow underwear with a long, preferably woollen *shirt*, covered by a number of thin *sweaters*, the exact number depending upon the temperature. An excellent way of keeping warm in winter conditions is to put a woollen sweater under the shirt.

Regarding *trousers*, jeans and cotton fabrics are definitely out. They have little insulation value (especially when wet), and corduroy-type fabrics, in particular, take ages to dry. Again, wool-based fabrics are excellent as they insulate even when wet, or you may like to buy a pair of *breeches*. Many of these are made from synthetic fabrics which dry far more quickly than wool, yet still retain a good insulation factor when wet. The alternative to trousers or breeches is a pair of *salopettes*. These are like a baby's 'romper suit'; their great advantage is that they eliminate the potential cold spot around the waist.

Some form of *windproof anorak* or jacket is essential. If this is not waterproof (and I mean *waterproof*, not showerproof), a separate set of waterproof outer garments should be taken. A lightweight cagoule is a good early purchase. Later, you might like to get a set of waterproofs made from Gortex or a similar fabric which, in many cases, can be worn as windproofs as well.

For cold conditions you should have a pair of woollen gloves or, better still, a pair of *mittens*. These should be large enough to protect the wrists as well. In winter, an outer pair of windproof mittens should be regarded as essential. You will also need something to protect your head. 'Bobble hats' or ski caps are good; woollen *balaclavas* are even better because they also protect the ears and neck. In winter conditions you will undoubtedly find some form of *duvet* (or 'thinsulate') *jacket* a great bonus.

Remember to take some *spare clothing* with you. Even if you feel you do not need mittens and balaclava when you set out, put them in your rucksack along with an extra sweater or two and, perhaps, a spare pair of woollen socks. You should always carry your windproof and waterproofs. In winter conditions it is worth taking a duvet or good sleeping bag.

Full length *gaiters* or the shorter 'stop tous' will prove invaluable in certain conditions, and should be thought of as necessities in winter.

c. *Food*

Always have a good breakfast before you set out. Your *packed lunch* should be nutritious, and you should carry something to *drink*. In winter, it is a good idea to take a flask of hot soup or something similar. Rather than stopping for an hour at lunch time, try eating little, but often. The same applies to the drink. You will also find it good to have a packet of nuts and raisins (or, even better, a dried fruit and nuts mixture from a health-food shop) which you can nibble throughout the day.

Before your first trip into the mountains you should collect together some *emergency rations*. These should be items with a high calorific value such as chocolate, glucose or dextrose tablets, mint cake, dried fruit, nuts and raisins. Wrap them up in a polythene bag, seal them with loads of sticky tape, put them into the bottom of your rucksack and forget about them. These are exactly what their name implies: rations for emergencies. The fact that you have sealed them well means that you will be less likely to succumb to the temptation of having the occasional nibble.

d. *Basic equipment*

You should obviously take with you a *compass* and *map* or maps of the area to be visited. Every member of the party should have a *whistle*, and should know the International Mountain Distress Signal (See Appendix I).

In snow and ice conditions, you should never venture on to the mountain slopes unless you have with you an *ice axe* and *crampons* which you know how to use correctly. Crampons, in particular, can be lethal if used incorrectly.

In winter, every member of the party should have a good torch of some description, preferably a *head torch*.

e. *Emergency equipment*

Apart from your emergency rations, you should always carry a polythene *survival bag*. This is a 3 × 6 ft (or 4 × 8 ft) heavy-gauge polythene bag which can literally save your life in an emergency. When benighted or caught in extremely bad weather, find some shelter, put on your extra clothing, put your feet inside your rucksack, get inside your survival bag and nibble at your emergency rations. The larger versions allow two people to shelter in the same bag, each person warming the other via body heat.

You should also carry a *first aid kit*. This does not have to be bulky, but it should contain a selection of bandages, dressings and plasters, aspirin, antiseptic cream, scissors, safety pins, etc. Group leaders should have a more comprehensive first aid kit.

In winter, the group should share between them a *stove*, a *pan* in which to heat water, and a good *sleeping bag*.

It is a wise idea for the leader to carry a 40 m length of 9 mm Kernmantel or No. 3 nylon *rope*, especially in winter conditions.

f. *General considerations*

Try not to be too ambitious too soon, and never go into the mountains alone until you are very experienced.

If the going starts to get rough, begin to descend immediately by the safest and most practical route. It does not matter if you come down into the wrong valley. Only fools press on regardless.

Always leave word of where you are going with someone responsible, and *let them know when you return*.

Never throw stones or any other object over a cliff or down a steep slope, and resist the temptation to trundle boulders. If you accidentally dislodge a stone, shout 'Below!' at the top of your voice. Whenever there is a danger of your dislodging material (when zig-zagging up a scree slope, for example), the party should move in such a way that there is no danger of any member being struck.

Exhaustion/exposure (mountain hypothermia) is an ever-present risk. You should know how it is caused and how to avoid it, and you should also be able to recognise the symptoms and take immediate action to prevent the condition from worsening.

While there are few objections to your wearing shorts and a tee shirt on good summer days, you should always carry your breeches, shirt and sweaters with you.

Always keep a party together. You should walk at the pace of the slowest member of the group.

Appendix IV The optical sighting compass

While it was said (in section 3.2) that the 'prismatic' type of compass was of dubious merit in mountain navigation owing to its weight and the lack of any inclusive protractor, there is one type of prismatic compass which is well suited to the task. This is the optical sighting compass from Silva.

At first glance, this compass looks little different from the standard Type 4NL. Indeed, the large base plate, which has a magnifying lens and Romer scales, is exactly the same. The difference lies in the compass housing. In addition to a squat 'dome', which contains the optical prism, sighting wire and the sighting window, the compass needle is a far more complex affair, consisting basically of a metal cross surrounded by a metal ring, the latter being printed with 'upside-down and back-to-front' numbers.

There are advantages and disadvantages in using this model. The major advantage is that it is far easier to take bearings from, or use bearings on, the ground. If, for example, you are travelling along a particular course following a bearing, instead of having to squint along the direction of travel arrow, then move so that the red end of the needle lies directly over the orienting arrow, and then find an object which lies directly on your course, you simply make a mental note of the value of your bearing lies directly under the sighting wire. Once this is done, any object which appears directly above the sighting wire lies directly on your course.

When using a standard protractor-compass to make a bearing on a feature in order to help you establish your position (as in a resection), you have to line up the direction of travel arrow with the object, then turn the compass housing until the red end of the needle lies directly over the orienting arrow, making sure that the direction of travel arrow stays in the correct position. With the optical sighting compass you simply look through the sighting window, line up the sighting wire with the object and read off the bearing shown.

The major disadvantage of the system comes when using the compass as a protractor. When taking bearings from the map,

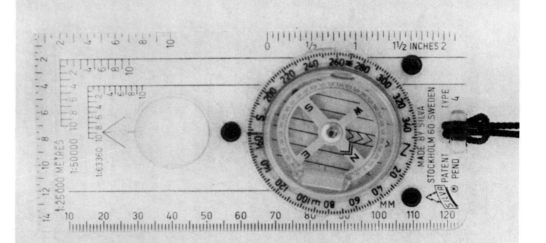

The Silva optical sighting compass.

because the large and somewhat more complex compass needle takes up so much room, it can be extremely difficult to accurately line up the orienting lines in the base of the compass housing with the north-south grid lines on the map.

One further confusion can arise from the fact that, while the divisions on the rim of the compass housing are, as usual, at intervals of 2°, when you look through the sighting window, the divisions you see are at intervals of 1°. Although this does mean you should, by rights, be far more accurate when following a bearing, you must always remember the difference in the scales.

You have a choice of methods when using the optical sighting compass to follow, or sight along, a back bearing. You can either use the standard procedure whereby you line up the southern end of the compass needle with the orienting arrow (difficult because of the format of the needle in this model), or you can adjust your bearing accordingly. This is done by simply adding or subtracting 180° from your magnetic bearing. If your bearing is greater than 180°, subtract; if it is less than 180°, add (e.g. a magnetic bearing of 27° gives a back bearing of 207° [27 + 180 = 207]. A magnetic bearing of 302° gives a back bearing of 122° [302 − 180 = 122]). Some people find it far easier to adjust for back bearings by either adding 200 then subtracting 20, or subtracting 200 then adding 20. You should use a method which you find quick, easy and reliable.

There is a fair difference in price between standard models and the optical sighting compass. Some excellent navigators consider that it is not worth the extra expense; others consider that the advantages of the system are indispensable. Ideally, whichever system you eventually decide to use, it is advisable that you gain experience of both.

Silva also manufacture another version of the optical sighting compass which includes a sighting 'mirror'. In general, there are not as useful in mountain navigation because the base plate is usually far too small.

Appendix V Useful organisations and addresses

When you first start to journey into the mountains, it is advisable that you join a club. Details of clubs can be found in the back of walking and climbing magazines, or can be obtained from the representative body of the sport:

BRITISH MOUNTAINEERING COUNCIL
Crawford House
Precinct Centre
Booth Street East
Manchester M13 9RZ
Tel. 061–273 5835 (general enquiries and membership)
061–273 5839 (publications, courses, etc.)
061–272 5163 (insurance, reciprocal rights card)

Details of Scottish clubs can be obtained from:

MOUNTAINEERING COUNCIL OF SCOTLAND
South Tillysole Cottage
Kinnaird Park
Brechin
Angus

If you are more interested in general walking, you might like to contact:

THE RAMBLERS' ASSOCIATION
1–5 Wandsworth Road
London SW8 2LJ
Tel. 01–582 6826

If you are interested in orienteering, information about clubs and competitions can be obtained from:

BRITISH ORIENTEERING FEDERATION
41 Dale Road

Useful organisations and addresses

Matlock
Derbyshire DE4 3LT
Tel. 0692 3661

Information about the training schemes and qualifications for mountain-walking leaders and climbing/mountaineering instructors can be obtained from the relevant national training boards. For details of courses run in England and Wales you should contact:

MOUNTAIN-WALKING LEADER TRAINING BOARD
Address as for the BMC
Tel. 061–273 5839

In Scotland, you should contact:

SCOTTISH MOUNTAIN LEADER TRAINING BOARD
1 Colme Street
Edinburgh EH3 6AA
Tel. 031–225 8411

Courses in various aspects of mountaincraft are run at the National Centres:

Plas-y-Brenin
Capel Curig
Nr Betws-y-Coed
Gwynedd LL24 0ET
Tel. 06904 280 (bookings)
06904 214 or 363 (offices)

or

Plas-Menai
Llanfairisgaer
Caernarfon
Gwynedd
Tel. 0248 670964

or

Glenmore Lodge
Aviemore
Inverness-shire PH22 1QU
Tel. 047–986 276 (bookings)
    047–986 256 (offices)

In addition to these Sports Council centres, the British Mountaineering Council runs a variety of training courses, and there are many other excellent organisations which offer holidays and courses to individuals and groups. Many of their addresses can be found in the mountaineering and walking magazines. The author offers daily (or longer) courses in practical mountain navigation and other aspects of mountaincraft. Full details are available from:

Kevin Walker
Laurel Cottage
James Street
Llangynidr
Crickhowell
Powys NP8 1NN
Tel. 0874 730554 (24 hrs)

Details about the Association of British Mountain Guides can be obtained from their secretary, Alan Hunt, at:

11 Dean Park Crescent
Edinburgh
Tel. 031–332 3468

Appendix VI **Further reading**

Mountaineering has a rich literary history. This bibliography is far from comprehensive, but it is hoped that it gives a representative sample of the types of book available. Some of these books are now out of print, but may be obtainable from second-hand bookshops or public libraries.

TECHNIQUES AND TRAINING

Mountaineering, Alan Blackshaw, Penguin, London, 1970.

Mountaincraft and Leadership, Eric Langmuir, Scottish Sports Council/MLTB, Edinburgh, 1984.

Mountaineering (The Freedom of the Hills), ed. Peters, The Mountaineers, Seattle, 1982.

Walking, Hiking and Backpacking, Anthony Greenbank, Constable, London, 1977.

Winter Skills, Rob Hunter, Constable, London, 1977.

International Mountain Rescue Handbook, Hamish MacInnes, Constable, London, 1984.

Safety on Mountains, British Mountaineering Council, Manchester, 1975.

Mountain Rescue and Cave Rescue, Mountain Rescue Committee, Stockport, 1985.

Mountain Weather for Climbers, David Unwin, Cordee, Leicester, 1978.

Understanding Weather, O.G. Sutton, Penguin, London, 1960.

Mountain Navigation, Peter Cliff, Cordee, Leicester, 1978.

Tackle Orienteering, John Disley, Stanley Paul, London, 1984.

Mountaincraft, G.W. Young, Methuen (out of print).

GENERAL INTEREST

Scrambles Amongst the Alps, E. Whymper, Ten Speed Press, California, 1981.

History of Mountaineering in The Alps, C. Engel, Allen & Unwin, London, 1971.

Annapurna, Maurice Herzog, Jonathan Cape, London, 1952.

The Ascent of Everest, J. Hunt, Hodder & Stoughton, London, 1953.

Space Beneath My Feet, Gwen Moffat, Hodder & Stoughton, London, 1966.

Mountaineering in Scotland, W.H. Murray, Dent, London, 1947.

Conquistadors of the Useless, Lionel Terray, Gollancz (out of print).

The Games Climbers Play, ed. Ken Wilson, Diadem, London, 1978.

The Winding Trail, ed. Roger Smith, Diadem, London, 1981.

I Chose to Climb, Chris Bonington, Gollancz, London, 1969.

Next Horizon, Chris Bonington, Hodder & Stoughton, London, 1976.

Everest the Hard Way, Chris Bonington, Hodder & Stoughton, London, 1955.

High Adventure, Edmund Hillary, Hodder & Stoughton, London, 1955.

Nothing Venture, Nothing Win, Edmund Hillary, Hodder & Stoughton, London, 1975.

Sacred Summits, Peter Boardman, Hodder & Stoughton, London, 1982.

The Shining Mountain, Peter Boardman, Hodder & Stoughton, London, 1978.

The Complete Mountaineer, George Abraham, Methuen (out of print).

South Col, Wilfred Noyce, Heinemann, London, 1954.

Classic Walks, Ken Wilson and Richard Gilbert, Diadem, London, 1982.

One Man's Mountains, Tom Patey, Gollancz, London, 1971.

MAGAZINES

The Great Outdoors, *Climber and Rambler*, *Footloose*, *Mountain*, *High* (Journal of the BMC) etc.

Most of these magazines carry stories, instructional articles, gear tests and surveys, as well as news and gossip. In addition to the pages of advertisements, there are usually directories of equipment retailers and clubs, and the magazines are excellent sources of information.

GUIDEBOOKS

Most of the mountain areas in the British Isles are covered by walking and climbing guidebooks. In addition to those published and distributed by major companies such as Constable, there are guidebooks of both a specialist and general nature produced by several small concerns (e.g. Heritage Guides).

Most mountaineering clubs produce guides to their local (or most popular) areas. Some of these are professionally produced, and distributed nationally; others may be little more than special editions of the club newspaper, but may still be on sale to members of the general public.

Details of all these sources of information can be found in many of the mountaineering magazines; they, also, often carry specialist features giving information about various areas, some popular, others less well-known.

Appendix VII **Permanent wayfaring courses**

Apart from those made available during orienteering competitions, there are a number of permanent wayfaring courses throughout the United Kingdom. These have been set up by the Forestry Commission and other organisations, usually with the help of the local orienteering clubs, and usually in scenic and fairly accessible areas. These wayfaring courses are normally open during the hours of daylight only.

In addition to providing a thoroughly enjoyable day out for all the family, such courses can be used to practise your map interpretation skills. Proper orienteering maps of the course (normally with a scale of either 1:10,000 or 1:15,000) can be purchased from the relevant forestry offices, usually at an extremely reasonable cost. As well as showing the positions of all the controls, they show other features which you can try to find.

If you are using such courses as a means of practising map interpretation, the controls can be used as definite features with which you can pinpoint your position. If, on the other hand, you are practising your orienteering skills, try to find the quickest route between the controls. In some courses there is a definite order to the controls (in which case, they are usually numbered); in others, the choice of which control to head towards next is left entirely to you.

The main wayfaring courses in Great Britain are listed below, together with the telephone number of the relevant forestry office from where you can obtain your maps.

ENGLAND

Ashton Court, Bristol. 0272 664169.
Cannock Chase, Lichfield, Staffordshire. 054-32 52082.
Chiltern Forest, Buckinghamshire. 084-44 6474.
Clent Hills, Hereford & Worcester. 021-354 3893.
Crowthorne Woods, Bracknell, Berkshire. 042-128 2801.
Dalby Forest, Pickering, N. Yorkshire. 0904 769290.
Downs Bank, Stone, Staffordshire. 063-087 2827.
Ennerdale, Cumbria. 0946 811130.
Hampstead Heath, London. 01-445 3106.
Hamsterly Forest, Durham. 0207 520473.
Ilkley Moor, Ilkley, W. Yorkshire. 0943 601124.
Lyme Park, Manchester. 060-430 2003.
Primrose Hill, Chester. 024-450 344.
Queen Elizabeth Country Park, Petersfield, Hants. 0705 595040.
Ranmore Common, Dorking, Surrey. 0372 52528.
Shotover Woods, Oxfordshire. 0235 20930.
Strenshall Common, N. Yorkshire. 0904 769290.
Whinlatter Forest, Cumbria. 059-682 469.
Whippendell Woods, Watford, Hertfordshire. 0923 43724.

WALES

Afan Argoed, Port Talbot, W. Glamorgan. 0792 23515.
Beddgelert Forest, Beddgelert, Gwynedd. 0492 640578.

Forest of Dean, Monmouth, Gwent. 0272 713471.
Gwydwr Forest, Penmachno, Gwynedd. 0492 640578.
Llantrisant Forest, Cardiff. 0222 40661.
Singleton Park, Swansea, W. Glamorgan. 0792 23515.
Westwood, Newport, Gwent. 0222 40661.

SCOTLAND

Beecraigs, Edinburgh. 050–684 3121.
Glentress Forest, Peebles. 0721 20373.
Kirkhill Forest, Aberdeen, Grampian. 0224 33361.
Queens Forest, Aviemore, Inverness-shire. 0463 32811.

NORTHERN IRELAND

Hillsborough Forest. 0846 682477.

Index

Figures in *italics* refer to illustrations or diagrams